Girls' Guide to Healthy Dating: Between the Breakup and the Next U-Haul

Girls' Guide to Healthy Dating: Between the Breakup and the Next U-Haul

Kim Baker

ISBN-13: 9781530101429
ISBN-10: 1530101425

For anyone who has had to start over

Thank you

to all my exes, who have been my greatest teachers in life;

to mom and dad for loyally commenting on my writing, even if the genre is awkward;

Ken for your everlasting belief in me and support;

Curve and Epochalips for trusting my voice in your publications;

to my readers for your support and feedback;

Jessy and Lisa for your amazing talent and vision;

Sam for seeing my original vision of SDWG;

Bixi for giving me my first opportunity to find my voice;

Brené Brown and Ellen DeGeneres for changing the world by being vulnerably and bravely you;

Emma for your loyal friendship and creative eye;

Heidi, Robin, and Vanessa for bringing me back to life;

to my San Diego crew, who has seen me through every single dating disaster—and loved me anyway;

to my amazing subscribers;

to my beta readers for your priceless feedback, without whom this book would not exist;

Steve at U-Haul for trusting me with your brand;

to Judy, most of all, because to you my answer is always yes.

About the Author

K im Baker is an online dating columnist, blogger, and educator who has been writing for the LGBT community for ten years. Often described as the lesbian Carrie Bradshaw, Kim redefines dating through the lens of mindfulness and self-responsibility and offers a new model for healthier dating. Connection is her principal value and the anchor for Girls' Guide to Healthy Dating: Between the Breakup and the Next U-Haul.

Kim is fascinated with all things dating and relationships. When she's not working or writing, she can be found reading, watching over the top humor movies or meeting a friend for cocktails and connecting. She enjoys running, spending time with family, dancing, and fashion. A Midwest native, Kim resides in Southern California with her partner and their codependent cats. Find her at www.girlsguidetohealthydating.com, on Twitter @gg2dating, or text gg2dating to 22828 to subscribe to her newsletter. Message and data rates may apply.

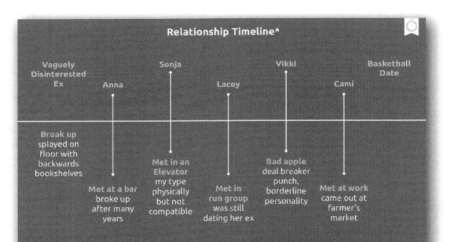

Relationship Timeline*

Vaguely Disinterested Ex

Anna

Sonja

Lacey

Vikki

Cami

Basketball Date

Break up splayed on floor with backwards bookshelves

Met at a bar broke up after many years

Met in an Elevator my type physically but not compatible

Met in run group was still dating her ex

Bad apple deal breaker punch, borderline personality

Met at work came out at farmer's market

*Timeline shows relationships as they occur in this book. For privacy purposes, actual names, events, and times are revised.

Table of Contents

Breakup Recovery

For the past hour, I'd been sitting on my wood floor, legs splayed to make room for the bookcase pieces I was attempting to assemble. I stared numbly at the half-put-together jumble of particleboard and Swedish instructions in front of me, realizing that half the shelves were facing forward and half were facing backward. I sighed, deflated. There was nothing to do but take the whole thing apart and put it back together.

I was a cliché for the first months of my breakup: a numb, expressionless, chocolate-chip-cookie-dough-eating, spontane-ously-bursting-into-tears mess. I went through the motions of separating CDs and moving out, and I spent weeks continuing to sleep neatly on one side of the bed. I began reading *It's Called a Breakup Because It's Broken*, by Greg Behrendt and Amiira Ruotola-Behrendt. According to the book, once you have figured out you and your partner are not on the same page, it is time to let go.

One message from the book sank in so slowly that I didn't notice it until it randomly popped up in my mind throughout my days: behavior must precede feelings. Even though I was beginning to measure my breakup progress by the decreasing number of times I cried during the day, the message stayed at the forefront of my mind: do good things, and eventually you will feel better. I forced myself to meditate five minutes a day. The meditation felt useless, as lack of sleep, real food, and a general desire to get up in the morning distracted me for the entire five minutes. I turned off the TV and went to hot yoga. I threw the cookie dough out and had friends over for tacos. I ran through the park. Then I went out for the first time since my breakup. I was uneasy and didn't really want to go. I knew I was supposed to seize my new opportunity at life and find my "inner hotness," as the authors called it. I did feel a lot of things—stupid, unsteady, afraid of becoming a lonely old cat lady—but hotness wasn't on the list.

I told myself not to bail on my friends and to have just one drink. Behavior must precede feelings. So I drank. And danced. And drank some more. I was so out of touch with being single that when girls talked to me, I looked behind me, thinking they were talking to someone else. I'm not sure "inner hotness" ever found its way into my mind that night, but for the first time in a very long time, I felt my smile reaching my eyes. I finally got the grays highlighted out of my hair. I started wearing clothes that matched again. Behavior must precede feelings. I stumbled, too. Ate a cupcake every day for a week. Drank too much. Listened to the Indigo Girls and The Fray. Missed a run with my running group. Was drawn to girls who were still in love with their exes, who had an athletic swagger and a tendency to be vaguely disinterested in me. I sobbed every night, burying my face in a stack of pillows so my neighbors wouldn't think I was being beaten. I ran. I worked. I refrained from drunk dialing.

And then, slowly, slowly, something began to lift. Behavior must precede feelings. I cooked using real food that didn't come in a box or a can. I started returning phone calls. I did hot yoga. I ran. I danced. I booked an adventure vacation for just me. I started a meetup. And I slipped. I cried. I went out every night. I spent too much money. I ate bar food for a week. I boogie boarded. I stayed home and watched movies. I engaged with people. I worked. I ran. And then one day, at my normal sob time, I noticed that not only was I not crying, I hadn't thought about my breakup, or how bad it had left me feeling, all day. An almost unrecognizable emotion stirred: hope. Since grieving sucked anyway, I chose to bank on the belief that healthy behaviors do indeed lead to feeling better.

This moment was the beginning of my healthier dating journey—this book is what happened next.

Old-School Dating

As I was putting myself back together after my breakup, I asked myself the age old question we have when we find ourselves single again: *Now what?* I desperately sought a book on how to date as a lesbian. *Girls' Guide to Healthy Dating* is a lesbian dating guide that transforms dating from an exasperating pattern of breaking up then U-Hauling rapidly into another relationship to a model for connecting with other women from a place of balance and authenticity.

Through the lens of mindfulness and the law of attraction, this book approaches dating with a focus on ourselves rather than on who we date and an attitude of curiosity rather than judgment.

By being healthier ourselves we create more healthy dating experiences and are better able to toss away the rose colored glasses and see women for who they are.

Girls' Guide to Healthy Dating is a call to courage for those who, after some years with the wrong girlfriends, suddenly find themselves once again trying to navigate the tricky waters of dating. For ages, women have gathered around restaurant tables with friends to begrudge the perils of dating as a lesbian, or old-school dating as I call it.

We date our friends.

We overstay our welcome in relationships that have run their course.

We pine over exes, straight girls, girls already taken, and friends.

We skip past the getting-to-know-each-other stage and rush into commitment.

My premise is something we all know intuitively: that in dating it is so easy to concentrate solely on the relationship that we lose ourselves in a giddy haze of infatuation, expectation, and projection. When it comes to dating, we can create a different experience for ourselves by developing a sense of self-awareness and by keeping our attention on the present.

This mindful focus is the currency of a healthy relationship.

Unlike other dating advice books where a relationship expert imparts knowledge on to the reader, I use a casual, Carrie Bradshaw-like voice to explore six powerful strategies for revolutionizing how we search for the woman of our dreams. I set out to examine my old-school dating beliefs and share my journey.

> *When it comes to dating, we can create a different experience for ourselves by developing a sense of self-awareness, and by keeping our attention on the present.*

So who am I to write this book? The truth is, I am not a dating expert. I'm not a relationship counselor, coach, psychologist, or social worker. I don't claim to be somebody who has it all figured out. But as surely as I know what I'm not, I know what I am: I'm every lesbian who has dated; who has endured the heartbreak of breakups; who has made every dating mistake in the book (or at least in this one); who has been single and thrust into the shark tank of the dating world; who has looked for the one; who has dated some amazing women and one or two shady women. I know well the patterns and cycles of excitement and exasperation that both tantalize and exhaust us. I know that unless we learn to look at them and ourselves differently, these patterns will simply happen again and again. If you see yourself in these pages, please know that you are not alone. Join me as we break some old habits, see things in a new way, and find real joy and self-respect in moving toward meaningful and lasting human connections.

This book is divided into two sections. The first section lays out the ways to focus on ourselves in dating rather than on others. In chapter 1, I'll show how committing to being authentic transforms dating from an exasperating pattern of breaking up then U-Hauling rapidly into another relationship to a model for connecting with other women.

Chapter 2 addresses the idea of concentrating on what we *do* want rather than what we *don't* want in dating. Chapter 3 is about how honesty can be a game changer when it comes to dating. Chapter 4 is all about connecting in the digital age and looks at some of the ways we can open up to new possibilities for connection.

Section 2 looks at the practicalities of dating and the unique challenges we face as lesbians. How do you meet women and hit on them with consideration and confidence? In chapter 5, I'll dive into some deal breakers, red flags, and other issues. Finally, in chapter 6, we'll look at what happens when casual dating turns into a relationship. Along the way, there are action steps that you may wish to complete. If one of these rings true for you, take it and leave the rest. I'll provide some useful links if you want to explore a particular subject more thoroughly. The appendix includes a fun quiz, some suggestions for writing your online dating profile, types to look out for, and a list of additional resources.

So let's get started!

Assumptions

To make my dating beliefs transparent, here are two assumptions on which this book is based:

1) Sometimes we need to just be with ourselves. Sometimes we need the time and space to grieve, recover, and stand on our own two feet again. That is okay and very healthy. This book focuses on the phase after that and is for women who are in search of love and want to date in a healthier way.

2) Having a girlfriend doesn't make us happy. We make ourselves happy. When we're happy with ourselves, when we're capable of caring for ourselves emotionally, economically, physically, and professionally, we are ripe for the kind of healthy, unbridled, fulfilling love that a relationship brings. This book is written on the assumption that finding love isn't the answer to life's problems, but is that amazing icing that makes life taste even better.

NOTE: I use the term girl or girls throughout this book as an informal way to refer to women over the age of 30.

Section 1: A New Approach to Dating

1

Changing the Focus

I pulled into a parking spot in front of the bar one Saturday night. Rain flooded the parking lot, leaving an inch of standing water everywhere. I put the car in park and let the engine run. Windshield wipers going crazy, I sat for a moment, peering out of the drenched, fogged-up glass toward the bar entrance. Still unsteady after my breakup, I felt uneasy even thinking about dating. I shook my head and eyed the birthday card on the seat next to me. I told myself I'd buy the birthday girl a drink and then I could be on my way home to my cozy apartment, where sweat pants, UGGs, and bad reality TV awaited.

An hour later I was sitting on a barstool, chatting with friends, when I felt a tap on my shoulder. I raised my eyebrows as the bartender pushed a beer my way. "Someone wanted you to have this," she said. I looked around the bar, hoping to make eye contact with my benefactor. Finding no one looking my way, I joked, "Well, I can't accept it if I don't know who it's from now, can I?"

The bartender tilted her head toward one end of the bar. My eyes followed. "With the hat?" I asked. She shook her head and offered, "Blond hair," before sauntering off. I smiled to myself, suddenly glad I had come. I stepped down from my stool and made my way toward Blond Hair, who turned to me as I walked up. I held up my beer and nodded. "Thanks for this," I told her. She smiled then, held out her hand, and said, "You're welcome. I'm Anna."

And there it was—the beginning.

Later, as I lay alone in bed, the dim light illuminating my mismatched sweats and stained running shirt, I imagined what it would be like to date Anna, to get to know her. A prickly fear stirred in my stomach when it occurred to me that for twenty years, I'd gotten lost in my relationships. It was like a horrible cycle I couldn't seem to break: go out as a single girl, meet, date, fall in love, commit, nest, break up, repeat. Who I was at the beginning wasn't who I was at the end. I wanted this to be my exes' fault, or the result of some relationship drama. But the truth is, I let go of myself because I didn't value myself enough to hang on to me. I believed if I didn't go all in, making my whole life all about her or about us, then the relationship wouldn't work.

Now that I'd met a cool chick I was already interested in, what I really wanted to know was how to date while keeping the focus on myself.

How Focusing on Ourselves Changes the Game

As Anna and I went about the sweet beginnings of our relationship, where my stomach flip-flopped whenever I thought of her, which was nearly all the time, an idea tingled in the back of my mind: What if our biggest challenge in lesbian dating is not finding the right girl? Instead, what if we're not spending enough time focusing on ourselves in order to be the right girl for ourselves? I desperately wanted to be my best self—healthy, brave, open, and authentic. I wanted to stop that all-too-common pattern of becoming the walking wounded, never really resolving the issues that arose in the last relationship.

I decided to start by focusing on the only thing I could really control: myself.

How to Focus on Ourselves in Dating

As our relationship went on, I couldn't help but wonder: Was it possible to remain focused on taking care of myself in every way—physical, emotional, social, spiritual, and financial—while in a relationship? Taking good care of ourselves puts us in a position of strength when dating rather than one of desperation. It allows us to be more emotionally available—that is, being present and responsible in our own lives, able to tolerate conflict, and staying open to connection.

If healthy dating means dialing in to who we are in order to know ourselves, be present, and own our choices, I thought, *isn't this actually a lifelong endeavor?* Ideally, this quest leads us to knowing our purpose in life. For me, the important piece was to begin examining more closely who I was as a starting point for this lifelong self-discovery journey.

> *Being emotionally available means being present and responsible in our own lives, able to tolerate conflict, and open to connection.*

Weeks later, I was sitting at brunch with a friend, and I asked her about her love life. "Women suck," she said, and went on to tell tales of her past few months of dating, which included being misled by someone who "wasn't entirely gay," being lied to by someone who "wasn't entirely single," and being hoodwinked by someone who "wasn't entirely monogamous." I took a drink of my coffee, furrowed my brow, and shook my head in empathetic outrage. I couldn't help but think about Anna. What if she was playing me? What if she wasn't who she said she was?

Later, as I went about my Saturday afternoon, I stood in the long grocery line and wondered: When it comes to dating, how do we pick ourselves up and put ourselves out there after bad dating experiences, without bitterness? How do we stay true to who we are so that we don't get lost in the dating shuffle?

As I loaded my produce onto the grocery belt, I distracted myself from my dating anxiety and played the *what if* game in my head. What if Madonna wasn't like a virgin? What if Gatsby wasn't great? What if Stella never got her groove back?

I chuckled inwardly despite myself and made eye contact with a woman in line behind me. She eyed my slow cart-unloading process impatiently. "Sorry," I mouthed silently. *What if Kim never gets her groove back?* I caught my foot on the back of the cart as I hurriedly unloaded the rest of my food, stumbling a bit. I could feel the woman's eyes on me. *I can't imagine why I was single so long.*

Later, tucked safely into my cozy bed and curled up with a book, a line of text jumped out at me:

> **❝ You get your confidence and intuition back by trusting yourself, by being militantly on your own side. ❞**
> **- Bird by Bird, by Anne Lamott**

I sat up straighter in bed and reread the sentence. I wondered if the way out of the bad-date cycle was to follow Lamott's advice. Trusting myself. Being militantly on my own side. In the end, no one really explained how Stella got her groove back. Maybe during this phase, we have the opportunity to turn it back around on ourselves. I recalled my friend's dating tales and wondered how we were supposed to trust ourselves and be on our own side if we were being lied to. I thought of my precookie-dough breakup with Ex and remembered feeling played. The thing was, I had known I was being played. I knew it even before I acknowledged it. Yet I hung in there, wanting to believe what she was telling me. Ignoring my instincts. Maybe that was my opportunity to stand strong in who I was and trust myself, to be militantly on my own side. I wondered, Even when we're completely caught off guard and not aware of the truth, can't we pick ourselves up with dignity, knowing it wasn't at all about us? After all, even in the dating world, where intimate relationships are so personal and can sometimes make us question ourselves, don't we know certain truths about ourselves? Isn't that part of being on our own side? Don't we know who we really are underneath the persona we show the world? At the end of the day, I knew certain things to be true about the real me. That was the girl I wanted to trust as I braved the trenches of lesbian dating. That was the girl whose side I wanted to be on wholeheartedly.

Action Step: What I Did

Determined to stay better in touch with focusing on myself while dating Anna, I tried a few things.

I read Brené Brown's *The Gifts of Imperfection* and took her course. When it came to getting in touch with who I really am, the exercises in the course did more for me in an eight-week period than years of therapy. Plus I ended up with a really great journal documenting my journey.

a. *I committed to focusing on my goals.*
   I promised myself that I would focus on my personal goals even while falling for Anna. I started pitching

article ideas to local publications, I paid off credit card debt, and I took care of a medical condition that had been plaguing me for years. By focusing on self-care, I was more able to be present and open to connection.

b. *I began to take responsibility for my part in past relationships.* Once I was in the habit of focusing my energy on taking care of myself, I was able to reflect on my past relationships with a clearer head. I became aware that I had a habit of being drawn to people who were only mildly interested in me. The challenge was compelling to me in some way. I had to accept that my attraction to vaguely disinterested girls was *my* responsibility. (In chapter 3 we'll look more at identifying our part in past relationships.)

Action Step: What You Can Do
Grab a journal and complete your own action step.

1. Identify three to five goals for yourself for the next six months.
2. Begin to examine your last relationship. Ask yourself:
   i. What role did I play in any dysfunction in the relationship?
   ii. What patterns did I bring that played out?

RESOURCE TIP: For more information about finding out who you are, read *The Gifts of Imperfection: Let Go of Who You're Supposed to Be and Embrace Who You Are*, by Brené Brown.

The Problem with Focusing on Others
How does focusing on finding the right girl cause problems? One way focusing on my vaguely disinterested ex got me into trouble

was that it redirected my energy away from the responsibility of taking care of myself. I put my energy only into the relationship. The same thing can happen when we're single and dating if we focus all our energy on finding a girlfriend. I could feel the beginnings of this with Anna as the weeks progressed. I was so enamored with her that I was blind to how things really were. I focused in only on the parts of her that worked for me and largely ignored the rest.

Focusing on our girlfriends rather than ourselves keeps us in victim land.

As I went about focusing on my goals, I realized I was slipping into old behavior. By diverting our attention and energy into dates or girlfriends, we set the stage for ignoring our own needs once dating becomes a relationship. A pattern gets established.

One of the upsides to focusing on myself is realizing that refusing to play a victim is my choice. Instead, I have to own everything in my life. For example, one of the ways I didn't stand in my own truth early on with my vaguely disinterested ex was by moving in with her too soon. I knew I should live alone; I felt it in my gut. But instead I opted for what appeared easier—moving in with her after only a few months of dating and basically focusing on merging our lives, rather than on examining my own life. In the end I had to work on myself while in the relationship, as there was no going around it. This experience was a good reminder that the easy way is never actually easy because in the end, when the relationship eventually ended, I still had to deal with myself.

Love doesn't make us stupid: self-judgment does.

It has been said that love makes us do stupid things. Maybe this is partly true. But when I look back and think about the stupid things I did to try to make it work with my ex, it wasn't love that made me do them. It was self-judgment. I judged myself for not being able to accept her inappropriate boundaries with her ex. I judged myself for not being the kind of girl who could just be cool when my girlfriend didn't seem all that into me. Mostly, though, I was afraid that if I ended the relationship, it would mean I was a failure. I was afraid it would mean I couldn't make relationships work.

Action Step: What I Did

Determined to watch my self-judgment while dating Anna, I tried the following:

1. I wrote down what it meant to me to take good care of myself, including goals, boundaries, time for hobbies, and priorities.
2. I visualized being in a relationship that supported my doing these things. This helped me to be specific and get in touch with my feelings.
3. I focused on how I feel when I am taking care of myself while in a relationship.

Here's my list:

1. *I will spend two evenings per week alone.*
2. *I will be brave with my feelings and won't make decisions out of guilt or fear.*
3. *I will continue going to the gym five times per week.*
4. *I will allow myself to make mistakes, and I'll be honest and communicate those mistakes.*
5. *I will socialize with friends or family twice a week.*
6. *I will honor my heart.*

Action Step: What You Can Do

Grab a journal and complete your own action step.

1. Identify five to seven things you would like to do to take better care of yourself in your next relationship.
2. Close your eyes and visualize your ideal next relationship, with your self-care actions in place. It may feel over the top, but the more you imagine the actual feeling of being in the relationship you want while taking care of yourself, the more likely you are to bring it into your life.

What I learned from my vaguely disinterested ex, from Anna, and from almost two decades of dating is not that I loved the wrong women, was that I focused on the wrong person: my girlfriend. I began watching my self-judgment and tendency to focus too much on the relationship. In the end I realized that I had more power than I ever thought—and the responsibility to stay focused on myself while dating.

One way I think about dating now is being comfortable enough in my own skin to sit across from someone and think, "Yep, this is who I am. I'm not perfect, but I'm pretty damn okay as I am." Most of us carry around some fear of not being enough. Not being worthy of love. Not deserving good things. Whatever our particular version of not being good enough is, acknowledging that it's there and looking at it without judgment can be incredibly freeing.

Focusing on the Present

It has been said that time is money. Where you invest your time is an indicator of what you value—your emotional currency. In today's digital age, what if time is only part of the picture? Think about how often you've been in a restaurant and watched a couple interact with their phones rather than with each other. On a recent cross-country visit with my nieces, I caught us hanging out in the same room as we all played on different devices rather than engaging with one another. It was then that I realized that today's currency is attention. Focusing on the girl in front of us on a date is the biggest statement we can make. It says, "I see you, I value you, and I am willing to connect with you." Time was the currency of the past. Today our biggest currency is attention and presence in the moment.

I will never forget the moment I knew. After some years together and a brief stint in couples' therapy, Anna and I were in the middle of yet another argument. I don't remember what it was about, but I remember feeling as if we were speaking different languages. Confused, I finally blurted, "Do you even care about how I feel?" Quite

> *Time was the currency of the past. Our attention to the present moment is our biggest currency today.*

matter-of-factly she answered, "Why should I have to worry about how you feel?" And I knew. Suddenly it all made sense. In that moment she literally told me she wasn't invested and didn't value my feelings anymore. There was nothing left to do but to begin the long process of untangling our complicated relationship.

Things didn't work out with Anna, but remaining in touch with my feelings meant I had to accept that I didn't like how I felt about myself while I was with her. I couldn't put my finger on it exactly, and I knew it went deeper than just blaming Anna.

With Anna and in my past relationships, I operated largely on autopilot, reacting to life as it happened to me. I focused on being successful at work, maintaining friendships and relationships, working out, and living a rather ordinary life. From the outside, all was just fine. But underneath was a girl who dealt with her fear of failure in personal relationships not by accepting the emotion and facing it, but by diverting it into distracting behaviors such as staying really busy, going out, shopping, and focusing on my girl-friends rather than on myself. The advantage of living on autopilot was that I didn't have to acknowledge my feelings and emotions—and the fact that I had no idea how to handle them.

After Anna and I broke up, I was tempted to launch back into the mode of staying busy and socializing all the time. But something stopped me. In the spirit of taking responsibility for myself, I realized that being unconscious in my life meant I often fluctuated between rehashing the past and worrying about the future. My mind was often busy. I missed many moments because I simply wasn't fully there.

When it came to my relationships, being unconscious in my own life meant dating women, sometimes for a very long time, when we weren't compatible. This meant not expressing my needs and then, of course, not getting them met. What I really wanted to be able to do more often was to stay present to whatever was happening in the current moment.

RESOURCE TIP: For more information on mindfulness and being present in the moment, check out *Coming to Our Senses: Healing Ourselves and the World through Mindfulness*, by Jon Kabat-Zinn.

Action Step: What I Did
Determined to practice staying present, I tried the following:

1. I took a free meditation course at a community center to help me learn the principles of mindfulness.

2. I downloaded guided mindfulness meditations and began meditating ten minutes a day.
   - I began to notice when I was distracted and not really attentive to the moment.
   - I began to notice when the women I was dating were not really present in the moment.

Action Step: What You Can Do

Grab a journal and complete your own action step.

1. Try a free, guided mindfulness meditation on YouTube.
   a. Start with short meditations; five to ten minutes.
   b. Begin practicing mindfulness meditation for five to ten minutes per day.
2. Throughout the day, start to notice when your mind is running and not focused on the present moment. Take three deep breaths.

Summary

Old-school dating is focused on finding the right girl, and it leads us to walk through our own lives largely unconscious or unaware of the present moment. The starting point for focusing on ourselves in dating is to spend our energy thinking about our own goals, taking responsibility for our role in past relationships, and being mindful in our own lives.

Perhaps the most important lesson I have learned in dating and in life is this: the more I know who I am, and the more authentic I can be, the more I attract people who support me, who bring less drama, and who help me grow in this life.

If we spent time getting clear about who we are rather than trying to impress women we want to date, we would not only be less likely to attract the wrong people, but we would feel less damaged when dating doesn't go our way. Once we've shifted the focus back to ourselves, we can focus on what we do want in relationships.

The more I know who I am, and the more authentic I can be, the more I draw in people who support me and who help me grow in this life.

2

Focusing on What We Want

A few weeks after the breakup with Anna, I stood in a soppy puddle along the freeway shoulder, holding my bike as rain poured around me. I had a nine-hour road trip in front of me, and before I'd even exited San Diego County, my bike rack, along with my attached bike, had slipped off the trunk of my car. Twice. After I'd run a sloshy fourteen miles before departing on said trip. This was how I found myself soaked and exhausted one Saturday morning. Zapped of any remaining upper body strength after a failed attempt to stuff my bike into my Civic's backseat, I stood in the rain a moment, looked back at the freeway from where I'd come, and considered turning back and going straight home. Instead I made one last heave, shoved the bike fully into the backseat, and pushed the door shut. Noticing the car's overhead light, I realized that the door wasn't fully closed. I shifted my weight back and forth, weighing the risk of driving all day in the rain with the back door not fully shut. And so, lacking any appropriate lesbian road trip gear, I took off my scarf, wove it through the door handle, and knotted it to the ceiling handle. The metaphor of a door neither open nor closed didn't escape my notice.

As I drove mile after mile along I-5, watching the wet landscape pass by, it occurred to me that the past year had felt much like my soggy attempt to close the door: with me wildly unprepared, tired beyond reason, and highly motivated to move forward. I wondered, When life throws you a curve ball, like when a long-term relationship ends, how do you move forward? How do you take all you learned in the relationship and move on without regret? Without judgment? When it came to breakups, I wanted to be the Jackie Kennedy of gracefully moving on. I wanted to be the kind of person who read my shelfful of books on equity in education instead of watching *The Real Housewives of Beverly Hills.* The girl who went to the gym before going out to happy hour. But the truth was, sometimes I just chose the least complicated thing.

Later, I got talked into meeting a friend, Tianna, at a lesbian event for the first time since my Facebook relationship status changed. I was uneasy and didn't really want to go, but it was easier to agree than to make an excuse. I told myself not to bail on Tianna and to have just one drink.

As I stood in front of the mirror getting ready, I felt a knot of regret in the pit of my stomach. *One drink and then I can leave*, I assured myself. Later, as I rode the elevator to the top floor, I heard music pumping and the sounds of chatter. I breathed in, suddenly catching my eye in the mirrored wall of the elevator as it came to a stop. "One. Drink," I mumbled.

Twenty minutes later, I found myself sitting next to Tianna and a drunken woman to her left. I stood, smoothed my dress, and nodded toward the bar. "Another mojito," Tianna requested. The drunk woman held up two fingers to indicate another for herself. I surprised myself by folding down one of her fingers, shaking my head, and saying, "No more for you, Drunky Pants." This made everyone around the circle laugh, and I suddenly felt more at ease. Drunky fake-pouted.

As I waited in line, someone tapped my shoulder. I turned and made eye contact with the dark-haired beauty behind me. I hesitated, thinking maybe I had cut in front of her. "Sorry, did I cut you?" I asked.

She laughed, looked down, and said, "Nah, you're fine here."

Nervous, awkwardly, I turned back around and mumbled, "Oh, okay, okay, good, good. Good." Suddenly I seemed to have lost all my social skills.

I returned, two mojitos in hand, and nudged Drunky Pants to move over and make room. "Ahhh, you're back," Drunky said.

Tianna and I clinked glasses and took a drink. She said something I couldn't hear, so I leaned forward. "What?" I yelled over the music.

"You look hot, mama!" She looked me up and down, and I finally understood.

I looked away and took a sip of my drink. "Aw, thanks. I was super nervous," I confessed. "I almost wanted to bail."

She replied, "I'm so glad you didn't," and we toasted again.

And then I looked up, and there stood dark-haired beauty holding a mojito out to me.

"I'm so glad you didn't too," she said, and smiled.

Three hours later I was atop a barstool in Hillcrest, surrounded by Beauty and her friends. My feet hurt from dancing on the rooftop. As I looked around, it occurred to me that while I still felt silly and uncertain, for the first time in a very long time, I could feel the light return to my eyes. I shook my head, rested my face in my hands, smiled, and remembered. There were photos taken. There were shots. There were hugs with Tianna and declarations of "I'm sooo glad you came out!" There were more mojitos, dancing with reckless abandon, phone numbers exchanged. There may have been some making out with Beauty in the elevator, and again in the cab on the ride from downtown to Hillcrest. I shook my head and mumbled, "One drink."

After a breakup, your past and present are like sumo wrestlers, circling round and round, waiting to see who will move first. Will the past win and take any chance at love along with it? Or will the present win and walk straight into the future? Dating again after a breakup can be hard, but it's really about moving forward and making our comeback.

Reframing Dating as a Comeback Story

A few weeks later, I found myself laid out sick on the couch. Weak, pale, and wearing my favorite feel-sorry-for-myself sweatpants, I was nauseated and anemic. Within a very short period of time, I'd been laid off from work and my relationship with Anna had ended. That was how I found myself watching Oprah interview Ellen DeGeneres. Oprah asked Ellen about the three years when she didn't work after her show was canceled in 2002. "Weren't you discouraged? Were you depressed?" Oprah asked.

Ellen adjusted herself in her chair and responded in an uncharacteristically serious tone:

> **❝ Sure, it was hard but I think when you have these trials that life gives you, it is an opportunity to find out who you are. Not just who you are when everthing's great, but who are you when everything is taken away from you and you have nothing. ❞**   *- Ellen DeGeneres*

I sat up. Just like that, I knew what I had to do. I had to find out who I was without the corporate title. Without the health to run half marathons. Without the support of being in a relationship. In that moment, in the clarity that can only come from life's hardest lessons, I began to think of my journey as my own personal comeback story.

RESOURCE TIP: For more information on examining where to go next in healthy dating, check out *Conscious Lesbian Dating & Love*, by Drs. Ruth L. Schwartz and Michelle Murrain.

So often we rush into a relationship and skip over all the getting-to-know-you stages of dating. In order to repurpose dating for myself, I began focusing on getting to know women. I created my own definition of dating as a way to check my tendency to rush.

Dating is the process of spending time socially with another person of romantic interest with the intention of getting to know one another to determine if there is intimate relationship compatibility.

Throughout this book I use the term *dating* to mean everything before a long-term committed relationship— from meeting total strangers to going out on dates to spending time with just one person while in a relationship.

Old-school dating often means not only skipping the getting-to-know-you phase, but also focusing on what we don't want. The problem with focusing on what we don't want is that we set ourselves up to attract more of it.

> **Dating:**
> *The process of spending time socially with another person of romantic interest with the intention of getting to know one another to determine if there is intimate relationship compatibility.*

The Law of Attraction and Dating

According to the law of attraction, like attracts like, and whatever we focus our attention and thoughts on comes into our lives. For me, this meant shifting my thinking from "I don't want to date any more women who are vaguely disinterested in me" to something positive: "I want to date women who have healthy coping mechanisms and who are as invested as I am."

RESOURCE TIP: For more information on the law of attraction, check out Oprah Winfrey's stories about living the law of attraction here: http://www.oprah.com/spirit/The-Law-of-Attraction-Real-Life-Stories_1/1.

Action Step: What I Did

Determined to practice focusing on what I *do* want in a relationship, I tried the following:

1. I wrote down five things I wanted in my next girlfriend.
2. I checked the wording for negatives ("don't wants") and reworded them as positives.
3. I identified the three most important traits.

Here's my list of the character traits that are compatible with me: *aware of feelings and capable of communicating them; able to work through conflict calmly;* and *sense of humor.*

Action Step: What You Can Do

Grab a journal and complete your own action step.

1. Write three to five qualities you want in your next girlfriend.

2. Check your list for negatives; revise them to what you do want.
3. Identify your three most important traits.
4. Take it a step further and identify which of these traits you have experienced before in women you have dated and recall how they were compatible with you.

Another shift is to approach dating with an attitude of curiosity rather than fear or judgment. It's easy to fall into a negative, judgmental attitude about dating. But by shifting to curiosity and thinking, "Who is this girl?" rather than "Let me see how long it takes for your cray-cray to show," we practice keeping focused on what we do want. Next, we can keep the "what we do want" mindset when we think about the type of woman we want to date.

Compatibility

Sonja was totally my type. I saw her across the room at a boring corporate party and was delighted to see another lesbian. And she. Was. So. Hot. I was focused on networking that night, though, and despite wearing my favorite sexy dress, I lost all track of her until I glimpsed her swinging ponytail near the elevator. I put down my wineglass and tap-tap-tapped across the floor to the elevator just as the doors were closing. At the last moment, a hand stuck out from inside, and the doors popped back open. We smiled at each other, and I was done for.

On our first date, I realized Sonja was the real deal. Not only was she beautiful, athletic, and a fierce businesswoman, she was also funny and incredibly down to earth. She was the total package. As we got to know each other, it felt as if we were made for each other. We were so compatible.

What is compatibility, exactly?

Compatibility is two people sharing enough traits, values, habits, and capacity for emotional intimacy and growth to connect and mutually support each other consistently. Compatibility is about being seen and valued for who we are, growing together, and supporting each other in our own uniqueness.

I believe compatibility falls into two buckets.

Shared-Interest Compatibility

Sonja and I had incredible shared-interest compatibility. We both liked working out, ate healthy, and valued our families and friends, careers, being out of the closet, and good hygiene. We both put honesty and kindness above success and ambition. These shared values mattered, of course, but they were only the first layer of compatibility.

Character Compatibility

How do we know the difference between shared-interest compatibility and deeper character compatibility? What you really want in dating and relationships is more than shared interests. You want someone who gets you, whom you get, and whose disposition, habits, and behaviors work well with your own.

As the months wore on, Sonja and I had a lot of fun together. But in the background, there was always an undercurrent of tension that I couldn't put my finger on. It was really confusing to me, as we had so much in common. We were crazy about each other! We were a perfect fit—on paper. We just never seemed to understand each other. Things came to a head one evening after

> *What you really want in dating and relationships is more than shared interests. You want someone who gets you, whom you get, and whose disposition, habits, and behaviors work well with your own.*

both of our schedules had been full to the brim for a few weeks and we hadn't seen much of each other. On our first shared available night, I thought we might have some wine, go to dinner, walk around outside a bit, and then head home. But Sonja had made plans to meet a friend at a swanky downtown bar, and she suggested I meet up with them. Then more friends would come, and we could dance and drink until the wee hours. I was so hurt. But when we talked about it, I realized how sincere she was in her confusion about my hurt feelings. We had such different ideas about what it meant to connect that we literally didn't understand each other's viewpoints. To her, socializing in a fun way with a group of people was connecting. During our relationship, we compromised some when it came to socializing. Sometimes we spent time alone, and sometimes we spent time in groups. If socializing had been our only difference in compatibility, we might have been able to compromise through it.

I learned from Sonja that loving someone is not the same as being compatible. You can't outrun incompatibility. You can't outlove it, change it, or fix it. No amount of good, hard trying will get you past the sometimes-inevitable truth when you just aren't a good match. Part of noticing incompatibility sooner, rather than many years into the relationship, is being awake in our own lives and accepting that while relationships take work, they shouldn't be incredibly hard.

Character compatibility is also about who someone is and how her character holds up over time and under stress. I see it like customer service. Say you're on vacation and there's an issue with your room. As customers, we learn to judge good customer service not when everything goes as planned, but when something goes wrong. How will customer service handle the room issue? In your relationship, how will your partner handle traffic? Family stress? A miscommunication?

Action Step: What I Did

Determined to practice focusing more on character compatibility and less on shared interests or physical qualities, I tried the following:

1. I listed all the shared interests that are important to me in compatibility.
2. I listed all the character traits that are most important to me.
3. I identified those qualities that had worked well for me in past relationships.

Here's my list of character traits that brought out the best in me:

- *Sense of humor*
- *Showing affection*
- *Being down to earth*
- *Respect/desire for me*
- *Independence*
- *Good boundaries*
- *Capacity for sustained emotional intimacy*

Action Step: What You Can Do

Grab a journal and complete your own action step.

a. Create a two-column table with shared interests and character traits that are important to you in relationships.
b. Note which shared interests are *must haves*, which are *would be nice*, and which are *not that important*.
c. Note which character traits are *must haves, would be nice*, and *not all that important*.

Attraction is important. We want to date someone hot. We want chemistry. That's all okay. My goal is just to not get stuck there. I now try to focus on who the woman is. That also helps me listen better and allows me to see her for who she is rather than who I want her to be.

> **Caution! Physical attraction does not a compatible partner make!**
> *Physical attraction/chemistry is part of dating. In healthy dating, however, it's just not first on the list. Focusing on physical attraction alone almost always leads to putting blinders on and failing to see people as they are.*

These days, when I go out, I try to dial in to how authentic I am being in each moment and how I feel around a girl. If I find myself feeling that old familiar confusion and everything-is-hard angst, I know I'm trying to force love over compatibility. What I've realized is that love doesn't trump compatibility. No matter how amazing she is, if I can't be me, if I don't feel I'm myself when I'm with her, she's not the girl for me.

Summary

Getting clear on the purpose of dating helps prepare us to take our time in stages of dating and not jump into commitment. Changing our focus to what we want for ourselves can vastly increase our chances of bringing that into our lives and is more pleasant to focus on in general. We are more apt to notice red flags, identify incompatibility, and get out and move on to the right one. Focusing on what we do want rather than what we don't want is more likely to draw in women who are on the same page. Approaching dating with an attitude of curiosity rather than judgment takes the pressure off and allows us to more clearly see things as they are. By waking up in our own lives and being present in the moment, we're protected from the blinders that love can induce. The hard love that I confused with healthy love in my youth is more like a roller coaster of inconsistency, worrying, or waiting for something. These disaster cycles can be addictive, and for many of us who experienced some difficult family situations growing up, these cycles are so familiar they feel like love. I had to accept that love doesn't hurt.

Changing our focus to what we do want for ourselves can vastly increase the chances of bringing that into our lives and is more pleasant to focus on in general.

In chapter 3 we'll look at how to be totally honest with ourselves and others and how this habit gets at the heart of healthy dating—connection.

3

Focusing on Honesty

I met Lacey through my running group just after Sonja and I broke up. Lacey smiled at me, and for the first time in my life, my stomach did a little flip. For the record, this happened once again about six years later with someone I wasn't at all attracted to. That was when I realized the feeling wasn't sexual—it was biological conditioning to human facial expressions!

Lacey and I flirted. I found myself with a crush so big that I wasn't even willing to find out whether she was a lesbian. Or single. I just flirted and admired her from afar, hoping she'd smile at me again. At some point we exchanged phone numbers and agreed to meet up for a run. Or a drink. A few weeks later, I woke up next to Lacey, tangled in the sheets of my bed after a marathon night of sex. I walked her to her car that morning, we shyly kissed good-bye, and I left town with friends. I thought about Lacey during the five-hour car ride. I felt so much hesitation about dating this girl. Was it fear? Was it my gut? Either because I was lonely or just wanted more marathon sex, I spent the return five-hour trip a few days later convincing myself that dating her was the right thing to do. What I realized many months later, after I learned that Lacey had failed to tell me she was still dating her ex, was that I hadn't been honest. I hadn't been honest with myself about not being ready to date. I hadn't been honest with Lacey about feeling uncertain about her availability.

Am I Ready to Date?

I began dating Lacey not because I was open, but because I wanted to avoid the restlessness of being alone and because I craved physical intimacy. Let's take a look at some good and not-so-good yet typical reasons we go on dates.

Not So Good Reasons to Start Dating	Good Reasons to Start Dating ★
Lonliness	Ready to connect with others
Anxiety	Feel solid in who I am
Sex	Ready to be vulnerable
Tired of being single	Healed from past relationships
Get over an ex	Accepted responsibility for past issues
Boredom	Desire to share my already fulfilling life with someone
Boost ego	Feel ready to balance focus on taking care of myself while being in a relationship

My rule of thumb before browsing OkCupid or texting a girl I just met is to ask myself, *Am I doing this because I'm lonely? Am I trying to avoid anxiety I'm feeling about something?* If the answer is yes, I don't make the call. If, however, I'm feeling solid in my own place and genuinely interested in getting to know her, then chances are

I'm acting more on one of the good reasons to start dating. What often happens if we start dating for not-so-good reasons is that we are not open to connection or we're prone to making poor dating choices.

For more on being ready to date or not, see appendix A for a short quiz. If you find you're not quite there yet, go back and read some books on healing from breakups and refocus your energy on getting right with yourself first.

RESOURCE TIP: For more information on getting over past relationships, read *It's Called a Breakup Because It's Broken,* by Greg Behrendt and Amiira Ruotola-Behrendt.

Part of U-Hauling into a new relationship is starting to date without resolving and healing from issues from our past relationship. In a sense, we haul all that baggage right into the next one.

Identifying Our Part in Past Relationships

I lay in bed staring up at the ceiling one evening, wondering about my role in the dysfunction and demise of what had been Lacey and me. In the past, I had told myself that I'd chosen the wrong girl—the "bad picker phenomenon," as it's called. *I have a bad picker. I choose girls who are unavailable. Who are vaguely disinterested in me.* But was I really taking responsibility for myself if I said my only fault was not noticing what was wrong with someone else? Was that just another way to deflect responsibility from myself and play the victim?

As I began to look honestly at my part in past relationships, I realized that there is possibly no bigger way to propel ourselves forward into healthier relationships than by evaluating who we were in past ones.

At first it was easier to blame Lacey for everything, particularly because I felt justified and righteously indignant after being betrayed. In our culture, we love to demonize. We love to look on as a celebrity rises into near-perfect-angel stardom and then falls apart. Demonizing our past girlfriends is a convenient way to ignore our own issues and play the victim. As my feelings of humiliation and bitterness toward Lacey began to subside, I realized I was demonizing her and leaving my own responsibility out of the picture. It occurred to me that it takes a far more mature, emotionally savvy person to evaluate past relationships with a humble sense of personal responsibility. I want to be emotionally evolved rather than repeat the same relationship with a different person.

Action Step: What I Did

Determined to learn from my past relationships, I tried the following:

1. I reflected on the five most hurtful events from past relationships. This included what was said, what was done, how I reacted or didn't react, and how it made me feel about myself.
2. I wrote a short story for each that began with "This situation reminds me of..."
3. I filled in the stories with events from the past when I'd had the same feeling.
4. I connected hurtful events from my relationships with hurtful events from the past that had resurfaced because of the relationship.

My example: *When I felt rejected by Lacey after she failed to tell me she was still dating her ex, I reacted by ignoring the signs and avoiding the conversation when I felt some-thing was off. It made me feel small and invisible—as if I didn't matter. This situation reminded me of the day of my parents' divorce when my mom drove away, and a few hours later, my dad and brother left to go camping. I stayed with a neighbor. I felt invisible, as if I didn't matter then.*

Action Step: What You Can Do

Grab a journal and complete your own action step. Since examining our own role in past relationships is such deep, meaningful work, I suggest using an additional resource as a guide, such as the book by Susan Elliot listed below.

1. Focus first on your most recent relationship and identify the three to five most hurtful events.
2. For each event, identify what feelings you had and other times in your life you had this same feeling.
3. Repeat this step for each of your long-term relationships.
4. Identify any patterns that emerge.

RESOURCE TIP: For more information on examining our roles in past relationships, read *Getting Past Your Breakup*, by Susan J. Elliot.

Victim No More!

When I got real with myself, I realized that my deep reaction to Lacey's betrayal wasn't even about her—it had reopened an old wound that had left me feeling small. To be clear, this acceptance on my part in no way excused her behavior or made it right. But it was the beginning of my learning how to stop being a victim in my own dating life.

Fast-forward a year, and my recent ex-girlfriend, Vikki, and I were stupidly trying to remain friends post breakup. As the weeks wore on and we hung out with mutual friends, something prickled in the back of my mind, an awareness that I shrugged off at the time as paranoia. The message was: *Vikki is dating our mutual friend Tianna.* This wasn't confirmed until I could no longer avoid the truth and saw the evidence that they were dating. I was devastated. Not because of Vikki. Pissed, maybe, as I'd suspected she was into Tianna before we broke up. But mostly I felt betrayed by Tianna. *Why didn't she just tell me? Who does that? It's against girl code to date your friends' exes, at least until they've been broken up for a while, right?* The worst realization of all was that in order to preserve my own health and well-being, I chose to quit hanging out with our mutual friends. There just wasn't anything healthy for me there anymore. Months later, as I cleaned out photos on my phone, taking a virtual trip down memory lane, it finally hit me. I drew people into my life who had poor boundaries because I had poor boundaries. I could continue to feel like a victim in this situation, or I could own up to my part in it.

I had no idea how to do it better. But I knew one thing for sure: I wanted to practice taking responsibility for myself. I had to ask myself: Where have I made poor choices?

Vikki seemed really into me when we met. Then suddenly, about halfway through our third official date, she was distant, a little condescending, and a bit shut down. I chalked it up to nervousness, as my ego wouldn't let me imagine she wasn't into me! Then, after attempting to date for another six months or so, she couldn't ever seem to find the time to get together. When we were together, I mostly felt she didn't want to be there. At last I figured it out—she just wasn't into me. Later I realized that when a girl wants to spend time with you, she will. Period. Nothing will stop her.

RESOURCE TIP: For more information on understanding the signs when someone isn't interested in you, read *He's Just Not That*

Into You, by Greg Behrendt and Liz Tuccillo. (Don't worry; the same rules apply when *she's* just not that into you.)

What I realized too late with Vikki was that it really wasn't personal. There are a million reasons why women may not be interested. Sometimes she is dating for not-so-good reasons. Sometimes she is into someone else and just going through the dating motions with you. Sometimes she is projecting something on you and not seeing who you really are. The way I understand the Vikki situation is that she wasn't into me, hence her pull toward someone else. But I wasn't honest with myself about it early on. Instead I pushed to date her and got my wish. Even if a woman isn't into you because of you, it's not personal. So you aren't her type. So what? It's better to know it early on than to invest years and walk away with a broken heart.

A lot of healthy dating is the balancing dance of staying neutral by not taking rejection personally and by seeing things as they are, rather than how we want them to be.

Action Step: What I Did
Determined to take responsibility for my role in past relationships, I tried the following:

1. When I looked at my role, I had to accept that just a few years prior to dating Vikki, I dated the ex-girlfriend of a friend. Then Vikki and I started dating when we were just friends—sort of moving from friends to girlfriends in one happy-hour daze. It shouldn't have

> *A lot of healthy dating is the balancing dance of staying neutral to rejection by not taking it personally and seeing things as they are, rather than how we want them to be.*

surprised me when she dated my friend. I had done it myself!

2. I realized the solution to my perceived problem of women with poor boundaries in my life was to set better boundaries myself.

3. I read journals from the time periods of my relationships and realized that in most cases, when I started dating someone, I was not in a good place. I was wondering, *Who would want to date this?* The relationship was just a reflection of how I felt about myself.

4. I identified ways I'd had my guard up in most relationships. I didn't understand for many years that my ability to be vulnerable or not was what separated true connecting from surface connecting.

Action Step: What You Can Do
Grab a journal and complete your own action step.

1. Identify three key ways you got in your own way in past relationships (e.g., you had your guard up, you started dating when you weren't over someone else, you moved too fast).

2. Go back to your list of goals for yourself and add one that incorporates how you can work on one of these aspects of yourself in your next relationship (e.g., I will check in with myself to make sure I feel good about myself before starting to date someone new).

I developed more communication skills and took responsibility for my own happiness. I recognized that losing myself in relationships was due to a lack of boundaries.

Developing Better Boundaries

One challenge we can have as women is setting and holding on to healthy boundaries. Boundaries are basically the borders that say what is appropriate and what is not. A boundary in dating and relationships is the mental line that marks where I end and you begin.

At one lesbian event, I ran into a friend I hadn't seen for a few years. In an instant, I knew she and her girlfriend had broken up—her girlfriend would never have allowed her to go out by herself. She hadn't set boundaries to maintain her life while in the relationship and created a dynamic where she couldn't go out with her own friends without her girlfriend unless she was prepared for an argument.

In dating, boundary crashers are women who don't respect the boundaries you set. Part of being more honest with myself is identifying what my boundaries are.

Some examples of poor boundaries in dating include:

- The girl you're dating acts more like a girlfriend to her ex (she doesn't have time for you but is always available for her ex).
- The girl you're dating suddenly drops all her other interests.
- The girl you're dating pushes you to have sex before you're ready.
- You date multiple people at the same time without communicating it openly to any of them.
- You date someone you're not really into just to fill the time.
- You spend all your time with the girl you're dating and stop working out or seeing friends.

Noticing

After examining my relationships with Anna, Sonja, Lacey, and Vikki, I realized I had terrible boundaries with women and needed to set some if I wanted to have healthier relationships. First I had to pay attention to things that made me uncomfortable. For example, I was dating Vikki pretty seriously when I became ill and landed in the emergency room. Later I realized that she'd had lunch with another woman down the street rather than coming to see me in the ER. That felt wrong. Maybe it didn't mean anything was going on with the other woman, but it meant the boundaries weren't great. My part in the situation was not allowing myself to ask Vikki to come to the ER. I didn't know about boundaries and was trying not to be "that" girl, the one who demands things of her girlfriend. But the truth is, I wasn't being totally honest with her by withholding what I wanted in the situation. In many ways, one practice in standing up for who we are is asking for what we want. According to author Mark Nepo, "The reward for practicing asking for what we need is standing in who we are, getting to know who we are."

Had I found the words to ask my girlfriend to meet me in the ER and she refused, that would have been information for me about her values and boundaries. Looking back, I didn't even know I had poor boundaries in dating.

> **Girl Code:**
> *I know it's tempting to date the ex-girlfriends of our friends but girl code suggests not going there. I decided it's more important to honor myself, my friendship, and my integrity than to break girl code and date the ex of a friend. Even if everyone else around us ignores girl code, we can still adhere to it.*

Once we have faced our role in past relationships and put better boundaries in place, we can get to the bonus of honesty in healthy dating—connection.

Focusing on Connecting

One afternoon, determined to get out of the house, I visited a coffee shop. As I looked around the bustling, cozy cafe, to my delight I saw cute lesbians everywhere. I smiled, took a sip of my drink, and went back to my laptop. I settled into my chair and thought, *Who says it's hard to meet women?* A few moments later, I looked up and realized that every one of us was on her phone, iPad, or laptop, or wearing massive, noise-canceling headphones. There was no way to find an opening to talk to anyone. I wondered, *As social media and electronic devices become ever more prevalent, is it even more important that we develop our ability to truly connect?*

I am reminded of a conference I attended when I was a teacher. During a session on science education, I heard something profound while the facilitator was discussing the effects of increased technology.

His paraphrased perspective was as follows:

> As technology permeates deeper into our lives, our ability to damage relationships increases. Consequently, our empathy, compassion, and thoughtfulness become even more important.

Similarly, in dating, as we use text messaging, dating apps, and social media as ways of connecting, isn't it even more important that we master the art of connecting in real life? Looking around the crowded, zoned-out coffee shop, it occurred to me that when it comes to dating, all that matters is how tuned-in we are to our own needs, to what's happening in the present moment, to who other people are, and to the ways we interact.

Being open seems obvious when it comes to dating, but in truth, how many times have you met somebody and found that she seemed rather shut down? To draw from the mindfulness camp, in order to truly connect with another person, we must be fully present in the moment. Making ourselves conscious to whatever is currently happening, including in our own bodies and minds, is the starting point for connection.

Connecting is what happens when you meet someone and that person *sees* you. And you see who that person is too. What you see is not some idealized version but a glimpse of someone's character, her heart, who she is. We can't possibly show people who we are if we don't understand and accept ourselves pretty deeply. As humans, we're built to connect. Yet we women can feel gun-shy about getting hurt once we've been invested in a relationship that didn't work out. A big benefit to developing healthier boundaries is that they protect us from being blind and becoming a doormat. This protection allows us the safety to be open and to truly connect with others.

> Connecting is what happens when you meet someone and they see you. And you see who they are too. What you see is not some idealized version but a glimpse of someone's character, her heart, who she is.

Summary of Section 1

When contrasted with old-school style of dating, healthy dating begins with a different focus: ourselves. By shifting our focus, we have more opportunities to take care of ourselves in healthy ways that are more likely to bring healthy people into our lives. Being present and staying open and honest with ourselves and others sets the stage for healthier relationships. A key to being the right girl is to first make sure we are ready to date. The healthiest reason to begin dating is being ready and willing to connect with other people.

Having better boundaries in my dating life decreased drama exponentially. I stopped putting effort into relationships that felt one-sided, I communicated my feelings when I felt hurt or confused, and I set limits with people. For example, when a family member was constantly late when we agreed to get together (like an hour late), I began to ask her to text when she left her house, and then I would leave, so that I wasn't waiting by myself with nothing to do at a restaurant or bar. With healing from past baggage and a healthy awareness of my part in past relationships, along with a healthy set of boundaries, I was more ready than ever to get down to dating.

Old-School Dating Versus Healthy Dating	
Old-School Dating	**Healthy Dating**
Purpose		
Short-term: Avoid anxiety or loneliness, get over an ex **Long term:** Settle down	**Short-term:** Practice getting to know people, decide on compatibility **Long-term:** Find connection with someone compatible in order to enter into a committed relationship
Approach		
Unconscious dating—losing ourselves or our intentions while dating	Taking care of ourselves while determining if we are compatible with someone
Reasons		
Anxiety, loneliness, ego boost, sex	Ready for and capable of connection
Feelings About		
Fast, hurried, anxious	Playful, slow, gathering information
Awareness		
What we don't want	What we want
Authenticity		
What will my date like most?	What will allow me to be my most authentic self?
Focus		
Finding the right girl Everything at once	Being the right girl Being present in the moment
Attitude		
Judgment	Curiosity

Section 2: Practicality in Dating

4

Meeting Women

S ingle in a new city, working and getting my doctorate, I found myself restless for human contact. As I loaded my messenger bag and empty coffee mug into my car one Saturday after class, all I wanted to do was go home, put on sweats, order takeout, and watch bad reality TV. But as I drove away from campus, I pictured the night unfolding that way and realized that staying home alone again was not going to get me closer to meeting new people. Plus, after a particularly brutal stats class, I could stand to blow off some steam. So I pulled into the mall parking lot, bought a ten-dollar shirt at H&M, put on some lipstick, and dragged my tired ass to a lesbian event.

From the moment I walked in, I was certain I'd made the right choice. I breathed a sigh of relief. To my delight, the bar was jam packed with cute women. Why had I thought it was so hard to meet women these days?

As I looked around the room, it occurred to me that our lesbian community had some unique challenges in meeting one another. Most lesbian bars had closed. We'd been socialized in a heterosexual society, where social norms told us not to make the first move. We often jumped from relationship to relationship, so we were rather inexperienced daters. Many of us had come out at a time when the world was a different place, and dating had to happen behind closed doors for fear of losing our jobs, our families, or being harmed.

Standing in the middle of this rare yet exceptionally crowded lesbian event, I was suddenly reminded of moving to a new school as a kid. When you move a lot, you become accustomed to lingering in the space outside everyone else. You stand on the periphery, observing the social norms, and try to find your place. Dating can feel like that—like attempting to learn the cool kids' rules while being a quiet, careful observer.

Hitting on Women

As I made my way past the overflowing dance floor toward the back patio, I was caught off guard when women began talking and flirting with me. For a moment, I was both shocked and overwhelmed by the attention. Suddenly self-conscious, I turned and made my way to one end of the long bar. After I stood there a few minutes, unable to get the bartender's attention, I realized that one of the women who'd flirted with me was ordering drinks at the opposite end of the bar. She was actually getting drinks served. It hit me that this was the perfect opportunity for a girl to hit on another girl.

As I watched, it occurred to me that the good news was that the bar was set pretty low when it came to hitting on one another in our community. Either we hit on one another poorly, or we don't hit on one another at all. We literally only have to be polite and sincere. Players know this, which is why it's a numbers game to them. They know that eventually someone will flirt back.

> *The good news is that the bar is pretty low when it comes to hitting on each other in our community. Either we don't hit on each other very well, or we don't hit on each other at all.*

Action Step: What I Did

Determined to take advantage of opportunities to meet women, I tried the following:

1. **I looked for access points.**

   I considered sending a drink to the other end of the bar, but I couldn't get the bartender's attention. I realized this was an opportunity for the woman at the other end of the bar as well. If she was interested in me, a girl standing alone at the bar and not getting served, she had an easy in—she could send me a drink. While I don't need a girl to buy me a drink, I recognized that situations like this one are access points, or opportunities to cross that imaginary barrier between saying hi to a girl and talking to her long enough to get her number.

   > **Caution! Sending over a drink:** !
   > *Some women find having a drink sent to them off-putting. Since it's a gamble, if you're not comfortable doing it, then opt for walking up and starting a conversation instead.*

2. **I put myself out there.**

   Later a girl walked past me, turned around, came right up to me, looked me in the eye, and told me, "You're beautiful." This stopped me in my tracks, and I mumbled an embarrassed "Thank you." I looked down at the floor and back up again to find her still looking at me.

   "I just wanted you to know that," she said. With that, she turned and walked away.

As I watched her go, it occurred to me that she'd done something no one does—she gave a stranger a compliment without asking for anything in return. I admired her guts. Even if a girl isn't looking to date, everyone appreciates a compliment. So I walked right up to her, tapped her on the shoulder, and offered to buy her a drink. In the end we wound up laughing and dancing until the wee hours of the morning. Dating wasn't in the cards for us, but we had fun, and I smiled more that night than I had in a really, really long time. It put my reality TV–watching, sweatpants-wearing homebody self to shame.

3. **I paid attention.**
A few weeks later, I was standing in a small crowd of women at a wine bar meetup. As I alternated between ordering wine and making my way around the bar to chat, I noticed that the women I was meeting fell into two categories: those who were paying attention and those who were not. The lovely ladies in the paying-attention group made eye contact, listened as much as they shared, and noticed social cues. The ladies in the not-paying-attention group were often looking around the room as we spoke, as if maybe there was a better option on the other side of the bar. They talked nonstop about themselves without really asking anything about me or answering my follow-up questions, which I asked out of politeness until I realized they weren't listening.

As the evening wound down, I found myself in conversation with a woman who was paying attention. I enjoyed chatting with her so much that I lost track of time, forgot to close my tab, and had to go back and fetch my card later. I asked her what she did, and she talked about her job. We maintained eye contact, navigating out of the way when other women squeezed past us through the crowd. She asked me what I did; I answered, and she appeared to listen. We exchanged numbers and agreed to meet up another time.

As I drove home, I shook my head at the recognition that hitting on women successfully begins with looking for an access point and ends with basically paying attention and trying not to be inappropriate. My next thought was that perhaps it is fear of being inappropriate that prevents us from initiating contact and hitting on one another in the first place. I sighed. I don't really know why hitting on someone feels so complicated. What I do know is that when it's done poorly, you feel oversexualized. When it's done well, though—why, that's the stuff good stories are made of.

Action Step: What You Can Do
Grab a journal and complete your own action step.

1. When you are out among other women, identify access points, or opportunities to meet and chat with a woman you're intrigued by.
2. Put yourself out there in one way each time you go out. Talk to someone you have never met. Ask for her phone number or to dance.
3. Focus on making eye contact and actively listening to women you meet. Identify when you meet someone who isn't paying attention and move on.

Social skills, like many things in life, exist on a spectrum. Hitting on women isn't reserved for the extroverted. Many of us feel nervous, shy, or unsure. When it comes to hitting on women, I believe where paying attention goes sideways is the blatant ignoring of social cues. As lesbians we can get it mixed up at times, and we think that if a woman is talking to us, it's a green light. But flirting is like dating—there are stages, and they are best not rushed.

RESOURCE TIP: For more information on the importance of initiating movement to meet women, check out the Gay Girl Dating Coach, Mary Malia, at www.gaygirldatingcoach.com.

Ten Tips for Hitting on Women

1. DON'T: grab her butt, breasts, or any other body part unless you've been given the clear green light to do so (e.g., "Don't you want to grab my butt?").
2. DO: pay attention, say hello, tell her she's pretty, admire her haircut, whatever. Be genuine and sincere—you can't fake it.
3. DON'T: call her baby, sexy, honey, etc., until given the clear green light to do so (e.g., "I just love being called baby").
4. DO: ask her to dance, ask if she's single, ask if she's been here before, ask where she lives, etc.
5. DON'T: say something sarcastic, inappropriate, or semirude to try to be cool. In fact, don't try to be cool at all. Trying too hard is impossible to hide.
6. DO: make eye contact, offer a protective stance in a crowd, lean in when she talks, and follow her lead.
7. DON'T: stare at any body parts other than her smile, grab her anywhere, or dance up on her unless given the clear green light.
8. DO: be yourself.

9. DON'T: talk about your ex or yourself too much.
10. DO: ask her for her number, card, or Facebook contact at the end of the night.
11. DO: give her your number, card, or Facebook contact at the end of the night.

Social Media

I confess to once holding a long-time crush on a friend of a friend of a Facebook friend. Her posts, pictures, and witty comments were so compelling to me that I made up a whole story about who she was. And then I met her at a lesbian event. She even flirted with me! She was all that her Facebook profile made her out to be. And she was also a little over the top, high on something, making out with multiple people. My crush came to an abrupt end when I watched her make out with a dude. That was when I began to examine my social media crushes. When it comes to Facebook, Twitter, Instagram, Pinterest, YouTube, etc., I'm reminded of a storytelling game from back in my teaching days—fortunately/unfortunately. Fortunately, when you meet a woman and exchange information, you can get a glimpse into who she is via her social media. Are her Facebook posts negative rants? Are her Instagram photos all boozy, partying pics? Unfortunately, while you can gather some information from social media, you're not able to get a full picture, and sometimes people portray themselves for who they want to be.

In the next section, I assume that, like me, you have tried meeting women at bars, meetups, the supermarket, book clubs, and other groups, or through friends. I assume that you feel a little lost, as I did, when it comes to meeting women. When a younger digital-native friend encouraged me to get into online dating, I resisted initially. I finally agreed, mostly because I needed to know there were other single women my age who (a) didn't want to hang out in a bar and (b) worked hard and were too busy for drama.

Online Dating

After much hesitation, I joined OkCupid and set my filters to only show me nonsmoking lesbians between the ages of forty and sixty who had a college education and lived within ten miles of me. I reminded myself that these were not character-compatibility markers and that I would learn more about our compatibility once we met face-to-face. But at least I could sit in my pajamas in my living room eating cereal and focus only on the bucket of actual dating possibilities.

I told my friend horror stories I'd heard about online dating, about friends who'd met women pretending to be people they weren't, men pretending to be women, nonsingle women pretending to be single, and so on. She shrugged and told me simply, "It happens. But I promise, the benefits outweigh the risks."

As the days turned into weeks, I found myself sitting cross-legged on my sofa, computer in my lap, thinking about my online profile as falling into two buckets: who I was and who she was. I set up my profile to address who I was first, followed by what I was looking for in a girlfriend.

Your Online Dating Profile

As I browsed profiles, it occurred to me that the rumors were true—many women were either so vague you had no idea who they were, or they told their entire life stories and their profiles read a little negative.

I decided to try an experiment to see if revising my profile would attract more compatible women. It goes without saying that the more honest and specific we are, the more likely we'll find a compatible match. That being said, I realize that there are extremes—the vague, surface level profile and the share-your-life-story profile. Neither are cute. Consider the following example from my first draft:

Your Online Dating Profile
Surface Level

I am petite, athletic, with blonde hair and blue eyes. I am a girly girl and love my shoes and fashion. I love my friends, running, staying busy, drinking wine, and meditation. I am an honest and independent person with a great sense of humor. I am looking for women who are fit, educated, fun, and confident.

I reread my first draft and realized that while the content might be accurate, it was surface level and overly focused on appearance (*blond hair, blue eyes, women who are fit*). While appearance matters, my sense was that if I focused on appearance, I'd attract women solely focused on appearance.

In my second draft, in an effort to be more specific and detailed, I wound up with the classic life-story version of a profile.

Your Online Dating Profile	
Surface Level	**Tell Your Life Story**
I am petite, athletic, with blonde hair and blue eyes. I am a girly girl and love my shoes and fashion. I love my friends, running, staying busy, drinking wine, and meditation. I am an honest and independent person with a great sense of humor. I am looking for women who are fit, educated, fun, and confident.	*I am just getting out there after of a bad relationship and friends suggested I do this so here goes. I am cute, girly, social, and have overcome a lot in my life. I have worked hard to get where I am and don't want any drama in my life. I am honest and expect someone to be honest and loyal as well. I like to have alone time so I am looking for a woman who can handle herself independently and isn't looking to latch on in a relationship. I don't use drugs or smoke, so please no drugs, addicts, or people in recovery! Couch potatoes need not reply.*

After rereading my second draft, I felt scared of myself. The profile said more about what I didn't want than what I did: *bad relationship, overcome, don't want any drama, expect someone, isn't looking, doesn't pressure, no drugs.* Even the positives were worded harshly! I understood now why this kind of profile sounds so negative. It sends the message "I don't really want to be doing this," and women pick up on that. I remembered the law of attraction and decided to refocus on what I did want.

Action Step: What I Did

Determined to be authentic in my profile to better attract compatible women, I tried the following:

To revise my drafts, I decided to be specific about what I was looking for in a partner and identify the most important traits. I wanted to stay focused on who I was rather than how I looked. I included only one sentence about what I wanted, but it was very specific and clear, and it focused on character traits instead of physical appearance. My final, somewhere-in-the-middle version looked like this:

Your Online Dating Profile ⭐		
Surface Level	**Tell Your Life Story**	**Somewhere in the Middle**
I am petite, athletic, with blonde hair and blue eyes. I am a girly girl and love my shoes and fashion. I love my friends, running, staying busy, drinking wine, and meditation. I am an honest and independent person with a great sense of humor. I am looking for women who are fit, educated, fun, and confident.	*I am just getting out there after of a bad relationship and friends suggested I do this so here goes. I am cute, girly, social, and have overcome a lot in my life. I have worked hard to get where I am and don't want any drama in my life. I am honest and expect someone to be honest and loyal as well. I like to have alone time so I am looking for a woman who can handle herself independently and isn't looking to latch on in a relationship. I don't use drugs or smoke, so please no drugs, addicts, or people in recovery! Couch potatoes need not reply.*	*I am down to earth, active, kind, intelligent and genuine. I guess I'm considered a lipstick lesbian, though I'm not fond of labels. I am outgoing but value time alone just as much. I am active but prioritize rest and meditation. I am a caregiver at heart and hopelessly independent and self-sufficient. I am friendly and social, but do best in smaller groups or one on one. I'm an academic and am prone to laughing aloud at stupid humor movies. I am looking for the one. However, I am just getting back out there after a breakup and so I'm interested in meeting new people and getting to know someone first. I love women who are athletic, kind, professional, confident, in touch with their emotions, honest, good communicators, and always growing.*

My somewhere-in-the-middle template is this: Here are the most important traits that make me who I am, beyond education, weight, or general interests. By being specific, conveying my attitude rather than telling it, and showing who I am rather than telling it, I was left feeling slightly vulnerable. But I was steadfast in being honest about who I was, so I decided that online dating was another opportunity to be completely honest about myself, which was more likely to draw in women who were compatible with me in character and not just interests.

Action Step: What You Can Do
Grab a journal and complete your own action step.

1. Revisit your online profile and check it for vagueness, negative tone, a focus on what you don't want, a focus on physical qualities alone, oversharing, or telling your life story, and so forth.
2. Revise your profile accordingly.
3. Be sure to focus mostly on who you are (as this is what the reader is looking for) and a little bit on what you are looking for.
4. Skim online profiles of women you are intrigued by and notice how their profiles are structured and how they read.

When it comes to meeting online, there is a lot to be gained, but it requires a lot of patience and resilience.

Technology and apps have given rise to some sense that people are disposable. After all, another potential date is just a swipe away. While this sense of temporary dating may increase the challenge in finding women who want to take dating to the next level, we can also use technology to our benefit by taking advantage of the upside of online dating: We don't have to stand around in a bar or at an event scoping out the room for a cute girl. We don't have to worry about unknowingly hitting on a girl who has a girlfriend and getting our asses kicked. Instead we can sit in our pajamas and limit our settings to prospects with real potential.

Online Dating Rule of 7

It takes:
Seven e-mails to different people to get one response back.

Seven responses to find one person you want to meet in person.

Seven in-person meetings to find one person you want to date.

Summary

As lesbians, we have some unique challenges in dating. When it comes to flirting with and hitting on women, it's best to be authentic and sincere and to pay attention. Online dating offers a way to sort through the important compatibility pieces to get started, but your profile is essential in making that experience a positive one. Once we start dating someone, we really have the opportunity to consider compatibility as it relates to warning signs: red flags and deal breakers.

5

Noticing Warning Signs

$\mathcal{I}$ remember it so clearly—the shock, the surprise, and the sudden sharp pain. I was living with Vikki. Our year of dating had not been perfect, but I was convinced our relationship was worth continuing. Then, in one humiliating instant, she had a flash of temper and punched me in the arm. A prosecutor might not label it as a felony, and a doctor wouldn't describe the injury as serious, but I was devastated. I had always imagined myself to be a good judge of character, but I completely missed the signs of aggression. In that moment it was as if all of the years of dating, all my mistakes, all my lovers' mistakes, all the pain of every fight, every breakup, every dysfunctional day with every woman I ever cared about, had come face-to-face with the realization that I had enough. I couldn't help but think, *Twenty years of dating, and this is where I am? How did I get here?* I was at my dating rock bottom. In that instant I made a promise to myself: *No more unhealthy relationships. There has to be a better way.*

I won't pretend that I bounced right back to the world of dating with a divinely inspired plan. It took time to regain my confidence, and it was time I spent coming to some difficult conclusions about how I had always approached relationships once I got into them.

Let me be clear that no one ever deserves to be hit. But I wanted to be the kind of person who, from then on, would avoid relationships fraught with drama. I wanted to catch warning signs earlier, and I realized that I had to examine how I had allowed myself to stay in something so unhealthy, unbalanced, inconsistent, and incompatible. I wanted to set better boundaries and throw away the rose-colored glasses. When it came to dating, my goal was simple: to be bravely and authentically myself while seeing others for who they genuinely were rather than who I wanted them to be. Step number one was to notice warning signs or red flags in relationships sooner than I had in the past.

Red Flags

When I examined my toxic relationship with Vikki, I realized that the red flags had appeared within a few months of dating. After a weekend at her house, I found my legs covered in flea bites. Not just a few—my calves had so many itchy red welts, it looked as if I had chicken pox. Still, she refused to take her infested cat to the vet for treatment. He couldn't have fleas, she said simply. And, she added hotly, if I wanted to "convince" her otherwise, I needed to show her the life cycle of a flea. Later, after the inevitable vet treatment, the poor cat crawled up next to me as dying fleas climbed around his eyes. The flea incident was the first of many times that Vikki was dismissive even when there was visible evidence of damage. One could argue that she also neglected her cat, a red flag of its own.

Red flags are whispers from our intuition that something isn't quite right. A red flag is that sinking feeling we get in our stomachs when something bad happens. They are slivers of evidence, usually showing up early on, that this relationship is not the right one for us. A red flag warns that deal breakers are headed our way.

Deal Breakers

A deal breaker, according to Dr. Bethany Marshall, is a personality trait or position on something that damages a relationship, that serves as a boundary for what we will and won't put up with. Deal breakers end relationships. Red flags warn you that deal breakers are looming. In my relationship with Vikki, the fleas were the first red flag. The physical violence was the deal breaker.

> Deal breakers end relationships. Red flags warn you that deal breakers are looming.

RESOURCE TIP: For more information on red flags and deal breakers, read *Deal Breakers*, by Bethany Marshall.

Why Do We Ignore Red Flags?

Over the weeks that followed, after breaking up and starting the moving-on process, I couldn't stop wondering: *What did I miss?* I had dated Vikki for a year and completely missed the aggression. Then another thought prickled at the back of my mind: *Or did I?*

The first red flag, the fleas, seemed somewhat minor. She'd insisted that the cat never had fleas before, and, given that the relationship was new, I swept the incident under the rug. But my gut told me something was off. There was no conversation, apology, or taking responsibility regarding the fleas. I realized later that the real red flag wasn't her tendency to be dismissive; it was that when she didn't understand my experience, she didn't care about it. This attitude showed a lack of empathy and is not conducive to healthy relationships.

Why did I wait to get punched in the arm before I walked away? Determined to trust myself to acknowledge warning signs sooner, I had to accept that red flags had appeared long before the punch.

Action Step: What I Did

To understand more about the red flags that appeared in my relationship, I tried the following:

1. **I identified when the red flags appeared.**

   Looking back, the red flag of the fleas appeared within the first month we were dating. More red flags followed in the next two months, like when Vikki disappeared for long amounts of time, was secretive about spending time with other women, and stormed off during an argument and then projected it on me, calling me a hothead.

2. **I identified the ways red flags got worse over time.**

   What began as Vikki's general tendency to dismiss my feelings escalated over time into controlling behavior that spiraled into contempt and disrespect. Looking back, the aggression was there very early. Several times in the first months of our relationship, Vikki stormed off and didn't speak to me for days. I need to be with someone who uses words to communicate. Aggression, punishing behaviors, and emotional shutdown are all extreme communication fails.

3. **I identified what was causing me to ignore my gut.**

   I thought I'd ignored my gut because I was in love. After more reflection, though, I began to understand that I'd gotten stuck in self-judgment. What would another breakup say about my ability to navigate relationships? Was there something wrong with me? What would it mean to be single again at my age? Self-judgment, especially when we're unaware of it, can lead to bad choices. I also opted for the illusion of a stable relationship over seeing things for what they really were. I realized that I'd made excuses for her behavior, such as "She's just stressed with work." I also believed her words over her actions.

4. **I identified the ways I'd allowed myself to become isolated.**

   I'm from the "don't air your dirty laundry" camp. The problem is that when my loyalty caused me to silence the truth of my relationship from the people closest to me, I missed out on other perspectives and support. There are miscommunications even in good relationships, and sometimes we need the support of our friends and family to sort it out. Being isolated meant I only had access to Vikki's perspective.

   I also realized that ignoring my gut had become a pattern. Once I'd ignored the first red flag, it became easier to continue to ignore them, even as they escalated and became more frequent and severe over time. I was so used to second-guessing my intuition that even on the day of the punch, I questioned myself, wondering if I was overreacting.

Action Step: What You Can Do

Grab a journal and complete your own action step. Since examining red flags from our past relationships is such deep, meaningful work, I recommend using an additional resource, such as one of the books suggested in this chapter, a therapist, or friend to help you.

1. Focus on your most recent relationship first and identify three red flags that you ignored.
2. Identify what you told yourself at the time about the flags that led to ignoring them or minimizing them.
3. Identify when the flags appeared in the relationships.
4. To take it a step further, repeat this process with your most toxic relationship (assuming it wasn't the one you just examined).

What I took away was that if I really want to see people and situations for what they are, I have to fully commit to experiencing people as they show themselves to be—in character, in action, over time. Also, I have to own the courage to walk away when we aren't compatible.

This realization goes back to what I talked about in section 1. Part of taking extraordinary care of ourselves is staying present, noticing what is happening in the moment with curiosity, taking responsibility for ourselves, and tuning in to compatibility. Another lesson I learned was to stop looking for things in places where they were not available.

To change this pattern of ignoring red flags, I had to not only spend time working on myself; I had to spend more time alone in general. Looking back on my few toxic relationships, I realized it was as if I had been standing in a bookstore looking all over for golf clubs. Worse, the mentality that "If I just keep trying, keep looking, I know I'll find them" simply took me further away from myself. I was looking for something that simply wasn't available. Some people don't have the capacity for sustained emotional intimacy. Sometimes women have larger issues that cause behaviors such as pushing you away after a period of closeness or doing something cruel after intimacy.

These days, I think of every moment in dating as information-gathering. If I have a disagreement with a girlfriend and she becomes blaming or aggressive or shuts down, that is information about how she handles conflict. Sure, everyone has bad days, bad moments; no one is perfect. But that's why information gathering works—every reaction, every interaction, is just information. With a firm commitment to see people for who they are, you will learn in time whether you're compatible or not.

My very worst relationship eventually became the best thing that ever happened to me because I realized I wasn't the victim. I learned that in the past, I'd wanted to be in a relationship more than I wanted to be in the *right* relationship, and I'd jumped in headfirst, moving bullet-train fast.

RESOURCE TIP: For more information on red flags and deal breakers, see *The Little Black Book of Big Red Flags: Relationship Warning Signs You Totally Spotted…But Chose to Ignore*, by Natasha Burton, Julie Fishman, and Meagan McCrary.

Deeper Issues

A few weeks after the punch, I was sitting at a restaurant table with several friends, sharing tales of our worst relationship ever. We shared stories of verbal and physical abuse, infidelity, drama, inappropriate boundaries with other women, lying, emotionally pushing away and then pulling back in, and more. I was astounded. We were a talented, smart, strong group of women. How did we get into these toxic situations and talk ourselves into staying, even when our instincts were screaming at us to get out? As I listened, it occurred to me that in each case, the worst relationship was different from all the others—there was something off about the girlfriend who was shadier than just being an imperfect person who had some issues. As I thought back on my toxic relationship with Vikki, I realized that she'd been an otherwise amazing person but was unable to let her amazingness shine because of her issues. I realized that seeing a woman's potential is not a green light to go headfirst into a relationship, and some people have more going on than red flags can explain. That may not be the right time to date. I somehow felt as if I was being judgmental by deciding not to date someone with a deeper issue. Over time I realized that part of taking extraordinary care of myself is acknowledging what does not work for me. I now understand that while we all have issues we are constantly working on, there are certain character or personality blocks that stop a person from being available for a real connection.

Other people's issues are not personal. They aren't about us. The idea is to understand what works for us and what doesn't, and apply our boundaries.

Action Step: What I Did

Determined to identify deeper issues that won't work for me in a relationship, I tried the following:

I identified the main larger issues that don't work for me:

- Addiction: alcohol, drugs, shopping, gambling
- Personality disorders: narcissism, borderline personality disorder
- Undiagnosed, untreated mental illness
- Lack of coping mechanisms: a tendency to run away or shut down in conflict, combined with unwillingness to look at that; uncontrolled temper

Action Step: What You Can Do
Grab a journal and complete your own action step.

1. Identify issues or deal breakers that don't work for you.
2. To take it a step further, identify ways you acted out a deal breaker yourself (e.g., you cheated on a girlfriend).

Among my smart, capable friends, in each of our worst relationships, we were dating the rare but destructive bad apple.

Public Service Announcement: Beware of the Bad Apple

Note: I am not a doctor or therapist, but I feel compelled to share my experience with a bad apple in the hope that it will help others avoid her.

It began with the fleas, and it ended with a punch. In between was everything from punishing me by not feeding my elderly cat out of anger to being inappropriate with other women. I spent most of my relationship with Vikki feeling as if there were something wrong with me or that I was going crazy. In some ways I acted crazy, and I got angrier than I had ever been in my entire life. I had a part in that ugly, dysfunctional, addictive cycle. After the punch, as I began to understand more about my own part in the relationship, I also began to see that this one was different. There was something really off about this girl, and once I started to put the pieces together to make sense of it all, I began to see that she was a bad apple.

The bad apple title belongs to a very small pool of women who we are likely to encounter once or twice in our dating lives. We may date her for only a short period of time, but the bad apple does a lot of damage, and it is likely our worst relationship ever. From my perspective, the bad apple isn't necessarily a bad person but, rather, a very troubled one who will not seek help. The bad apple is more than someone who makes mistakes; we're all imperfect. The bad apple has deeper issues than most people do, character issues that will make the apple rot. I'm referring to those people who have personality disorders, primarily narcissistic personality disorder and borderline personality disorder. If you spend enough time with someone like this, you'll feel yourself getting sucked into a toxic cycle of drama. The bad apple shows a pattern of behavior that is bizarre and inappropriate, and it leaves you wondering if you're crazy.

Action Step: What I Did

Determined to identify personality issues sooner, I tried the following:

1. **I identified how to spot a bad apple.**
   We all have our own ideas of what defines a bad apple. In an effort to understand more, I researched personality disorder symptoms. I felt better when I realized the behavior had a name and a set of common symptoms, and it helped me understand the problems in the relationship weren't all on me.

   Some general behaviors that I have found to be consistent among all bad apples include
   - idealizing you or being overly seductive in the beginning,
   - believing people are all bad or all good,
   - not taking any responsibility for things,
   - exhibiting punishing behavior when you do something she disagrees with,
   - behaving impulsively; maybe having addiction issues,

⟩ experiencing extreme mood swings—Jekyll and Hyde,

⟩ blaming; is always the victim,

⟩ pushing you away and pulling you back in,

⟩ expressing little emotion during conflict, particularly when you're upset,

⟩ not reacting like most people in similar situations,

⟩ exhibiting behavior that makes you feel crazy,

⟩ losing interest in you once you're interested in her,

⟩ preying on people, and

⟩ exhibiting controlling behavior.

2. **I accepted that it's not my job to help a bad apple.** I would wither away from pessimism if I didn't believe that it's never too late for people to change. Now I understand that it's not up to me to help broken women, and healing doesn't have to happen on my watch. The thing about many with personality disorders such as borderline personality disorder is that they very rarely get treatment. I had to accept that part of the illness is unwillingness or incapacity for self-insight. Spending time trying to help someone in this camp, in my experience, is like pouring energy down a bottomless pit.

Action Step: What You Can Do

Grab a journal and complete your own action step. Since bad apples, or people who have personality disorders, are complex, I recommend consulting an additional resource, such as one of the books recommended in this chapter or a therapist, to help you.

1. Thank your lucky stars if you have never dated one. Or

2. Identify one bad apple you have dated.

3. Identify the symptoms or signs that there was something off about her—more than just being an imperfect human being.

4. Identify what you told yourself about these signs that allowed you to stay in the relationship.

5. To take it a step further, identify what events or feelings from your past were similar, as these can become hooks that keep us in an addicted-like state with a bad apple.

6. Forgive yourself. Accept that you did the best you could. Forgive her, and accept that she is not well and did the best she could. Focus your energy on learning to trust your own judgment again.

From my perspective, since everyone exhibits some of the above behaviors occasionally, particularly in conflict, the biggest thing to watch for is a pattern of these behaviors over a period of time. We all go through transitions and make poor choices. What differentiates a bad apple from a regular apple are those behaviors over a period of time.

RESOURCE TIP: For more information on personality disorders, see *Women Who Love Psychopaths*, by Sandra L. Brown.

Fortunately, the bad apple is rare. What is more common in dating is meeting women who have general behaviors that don't work well for many people in relationships. See appendix C for more about these types.

> **Girl Code:**
> *We want to be good friends and not say anything bad about our friends' girlfriends. But how many times after a breakup have you heard your friends say, "I never liked how she treated you," and you were shocked they never said anything? Maybe there is a middle ground available, between saying nothing at all when we see red flags or issues, and saying we hate her.*

When it comes to dating, you truly don't know someone's character until you know it. The main thing to do when we sense that something isn't right is to watch it over time. It's about patterns over time and over different circumstances, patterns during conflict and stress, and inability for personal growth.

Love

Once I fell in love, too often I got a little lost or blind to things as they were. I ignored red flags, compromised on my deal breakers, and, in one case, tolerated a bad apple until I got hit. Because of my tendency to ignore reality when in love, I considered what love is and what it isn't.

What Love Is and Is Not

I sat at a table in a bar, along with four married friends, in between happy hour and the late hours reserved for the younger crowd. I noticed we were all talking about the same thing: relationships and dating. The two ladies who had been in the longest relationships had the same theme: "I didn't know it could be this easy." I found myself nodding as I sipped my vodka. When did we start believing dating had to be so hard? And does it? I listened curiously as my friends described their relationships in the early stages—the first dates, the milestones such as meeting family—and I chuckled as they shared their amazement at how they kept waiting for the other shoe to drop. Yet it never did. Stuff came up. There were misses, small breaks in the relationship. But then there was communication, repair, and reconnection. For the most part, the misses were few and far between—and far from any deal breakers.

In my worst relationship, I spent a lot of time convincing my friends I was happy. I spent a lot of time waiting around for Her. For Her to get ready. For Her to show up. For Her to come home. For Her to answer a text message. For Her to talk to me. For Her to own up to anything, as she seemed capable of owning up to virtually nothing, at least not out loud. I remember the duality of my heart the weekend we moved in together, when we sat in separate rooms, not speaking. There might as well have been a continent between us. Sometimes I actually wondered, *Do I still have a girlfriend? And if so, where the hell is she?* I realized that once you start trying to convince people that you're happy, you're not happy.

This relationship wasn't love. It was attachment, and maybe caring on some level. But all of the misses, disrespect, and contempt were not indicators of love.

In *Getting Past Your Breakup*, Susan Elliot explains that love doesn't hurt:

> ⟩ Love isn't passive aggressive—it doesn't push you away and pull you back in.

- Love doesn't cause you to lose things—friends, sleep, hobbies, appetite, or health.
- Love doesn't make you wait, worry, or wonder.
- Love doesn't need to apologize very often but will when it's necessary.

Action Step: What I Did

Determined to identify sooner what love is and is not, I tried the following:

Based on Elliot's descriptions of what love is not, I created a checklist for myself to lean against when I fall in love.

Is this love?
☐ Is she consistent?
☐ Is she kind/loving?
☐ Can she communicate?
☐ Does she make your life better?
☐ Do you rarely worry, wait, wonder what will happen?
☐ Do you keep your voice, your friends, your health, your sleep, your appetite?
☐ Is it easy most of the time?
☐ Does it not hurt?
☐ Are you focused on you?
☐ Do her actions show love?
☐ Are you accepted and loved for who you are?
☐ Can you be yourself?
☐ Does she make your life larger?
☐ Do you feel seen, heard, and valued?

Summary

Dating can feel hard enough, but being able to identify red flags, deal breakers, and issues can help us get out of unhealthy relationships sooner. We should be mindful that while most women are good people, there are a few bad apples out there who have deeper issues or disorders that prevent them from having healthy relationships. Once we've navigated some challenges in dating, we are ready for the sweet stuff: dating that becomes a relationship.

6

Dating That Becomes a Relationship

There are plenty of great relationship books out there, and I don't attempt to examine long-term relationships thoroughly in this book. But I want to address navigating dating that becomes a long-term relationship because much of a relationship *is* dating—it's just dating one person.

My wild summer came to an abrupt end when I met Cami. I was minding my own dating-but-not-getting-attached-to-anyone business when *wham*! Cami walked into my office at work and introduced herself as a consultant working with our marketing department, and I was done for. Wild summer—out. She was smart, professional, and everything I was looking for in a girlfriend. After we had seen each other a few weekends in the midst of her very busy travel schedule, I was smitten. Trouble was, I had no idea if she felt the same. Then one evening, as we chatted about our days, she told me about how a woman had hit on her, and Cami told her she already had a girlfriend. I froze. Had she just called me her girlfriend? Part of me was thrilled. This was what I wanted. The other part of me was confused—when had we decided to be girlfriends? Had we?

How Do I Know I'm in a Relationship?

If dating is spending time with a romantic interest to determine whether there is intimate compatibility or not, then what is a relationship? For the purposes of this book, I refer to a relationship as an intimate, romantic, monogamous, sexual relationship between two people. I have used the terms "dating" and "relationship" interchangeably throughout this book because even when we're in a relationship, we are still dating. Moving from just dating to being-in-a-relationship dating is all about the conversation. At some point I realized I was into Cami and wanted to spend time with only her, and I needed to tell her how I felt.

> *Moving from just dating to being-in-a-relationship dating is all about the conversation.*

Action Step: What I Did

Determined to communicate honestly and clearly, I tried the following:

I had a conversation with Cami.

In the spirit of being totally honest with myself and Cami, I decided to become really clear about where we stood. I wanted to know if we were dating only each other, and if so, what that meant. During our conversation, we each talked about what we wanted, and we agreed on some parameters.

Action Step: What You Can Do

Grab a journal and complete your own action step.

1. If you are dating women, identify two ways you can bring more honesty to the situation(s).

2. Identify one situation from the past where you could have been more open and honest.

3. Set a specific goal for going forward related to step 2 (e.g., going forward, I will tell women I date from the start that I am dating other women).

Relationship-Dating Milestones

Dating is like one of those sandbox sifter toys that trap bigger pebbles and gravel and allow finer grains of sand to pass through. In dating, the big stuff is more obvious earlier in the relationship, usually by the three-month mark. Once all the big chunks of gravel are out of the way, you can more easily see the medium-sized pebbles, usually by the six-month mark. Around nine months, the smaller, finer grains reveal themselves. By the time you've been dating one year, you can look at the whole pile and ask yourself: Is this the relationship I want to be in? Will it work for me?

Action Step: What I Did

Determined to identify compatibility and incompatibility sooner, I tried the following:

I created an internal visual to help me understand the phases of relationship dating.

1. **Phase one: three months.** Big issues will show up—temper, emotional and mental stability, drugs/alcohol, character issues. Red flags will make at least one appearance.

2. **Phase two: six months.** All of the above and finer compatibility issues will appear—social behaviors, busy schedules, work, exercise and self-care, organization, cleanliness and communication styles—and red flags

will have arisen multiple times. You may be wondering about deal breakers.

3. **Phase three: nine months.** All of the above and the finer compatibility markers will appear—goals, family, the need for socializing versus alone time, consistency, how you communicate in conflict, and money. Your gut will be telling you something if this is not the right relationship for you. Your deal breakers are screaming at you.

4. **Phase four: one year.** All of the above will appear, and this is the point where you can look at the whole picture of the person and determine whether this is a healthy relationship for you. This is the time to consider moving in, committing to a long-term relationship, planning a big vacation, or making a major purchase together. You will not be able to continue the status quo if this is not the right relationship for you.

Action Step: What You Can Do
Grab a journal and complete your own action step.

1. Focus on your most recent relationship first and identify the specific timing of when you noticed things.
2. To take it a step further, identify what you told yourself at the time.
3. Set the intention to put your mind in a curious, information-gathering mind-set rather than judgment.

Isn't a year a long time to wait to see whether we're compatible or not? The truth is, it simply takes time to get to know each other. By going back to an ex, I know what I'm working with; I've already invested a certain amount of time in the relationship. By staying single, I choose to invest the time in myself alone. Both of those options are perfectly appropriate. I have chosen both at different points in my life. But eventually I was ready to enter into a healthy partnership again, knowing that it would take some time to sift the grains of sand and to practice seeing the truth without judgment and weighing whether it would work for me or not. Bottom line: you simply can't rush the sifting-sand timeline.

Exceptions

There are some situations that extend the sifting-sand timeline beyond the one-year mark. Under some circumstances, you may be nine months into the relationship, but it's really as if you're at the three-month point. It's best to be mindful that it may take a little longer to determine compatibility in some situations, such as the following:

- Long-distance relationships
- Major life events (job disruptions, death, illness)
- Personality issues (narcissism, borderline personality)
- Drug/alcohol addictions (including being sober but not treating the cause of the addiction)
- Going back to school, moving, work, travel (or anything that creates ultrabusy schedules)

Dating Obstacles

In chapter 5 I addressed unique challenges for lesbians. Here I address obstacles that can happen in any dating situation.

Timing

There is a saying that goes, "If the timing is wrong, the girl is wrong." There are all kinds of timing issues that can come up.

Keep in mind that not everyone out there is ready to date, although they may not be aware that they aren't ready. Some indicators that someone isn't ready are the following:

- Giving I-don't-want-a-girlfriend signals
- Sending mixed or inconsistent messages
- Not being over an ex
- Literally saying, "I don't want to hurt you"
- Never having time for you
- Being unable to be present
- Being unable to manage emotions or stress

Long-Distance Relationships

Deciding whether to get into a long-distance dating relationship or not is really about knowing yourself. In my experience, if I leave it up to chance, I'll wind up in a long-distance relationship even though I've sworn to myself I'd never do it again. I've decided they don't work for me. But if you're open to a long-distance relationship, it might be good to decide how far you're comfortable traveling and how long you're willing to commute in order to date. I know many happily partnered couples who began long distance. It worked for them because each person knew what she could deal with, and they communicated that with each other.

Ghosts of Girlfriends Past

Since we often stay quite close with exes, particularly those from many years ago, how can we deal with a girlfriend's ex in a healthy way? For one, the truth is that if your girlfriend's ex is still close with her, chances are very high that the ex is in fact a good person. Why else would your girlfriend permit that closeness? Banking on that belief, then, one approach is to be open to getting to know the ex, keeping in mind that she may be particularly protective of your girlfriend. It may take a while to get to know each other, and that's okay. In the meantime, it's okay to notice and have feelings about things that seem odd. The key, as in many other parts of dating, lies in boundaries. For example, some red flags I experienced when it comes to exes are as follows:

- Your girlfriend either always talks about her ex, or she won't say her name at all and avoids the subject when you bring it up.
- Your girlfriend ditches you when you're all together.
- Your girlfriend is overly defensive about their friendship, putting it mostly on you to "make nice."
- Your girlfriend is jealous of your exes.
- Your girlfriend prioritizes her ex over you (e.g., takes her calls during the workday but is too busy to take your call).
- There are ghosts of ex-girlfriends all over her home— vacation photos, pictures on the fridge, jewelry, etc.

Flags aside, we can have perfectly appropriate, healthy relationships with our exes. In our community, exes are simply part of our lives, whether we like it or not. The best thing is to keep an eye on boundaries—your own, your exes', your girlfriend's, her exes'. You'll know in your gut if something feels off. This off feeling is a red flag.

One last note on exes: when it comes to dating and your own ex, beware of the law of exes.

> **Caution! The Law of Exes:** !
> *The law of exes states that there is a direct correlation between how good you feel and the positive interest your ex shows in you. In short, the very moment you start to move on, your ex will reappear in some way. Do not let the law of exes stop you from your new, amazing dating life! Your best defense is to be aware of the law and expect it to happen.*

Relationship Milestones

Sex

There is some nebulous three-date rule when it comes to sex. I have had sex on the first date; I have had sex on the third date. And a few times I have waited until around date nine or ten, partly inspired by *The Forty-Year-Old Virgin*. I realize this is weird. But we all say we want to take things slowly. We tell ourselves to go slowly. But we like sex. Particularly when we haven't had it in a while, we just want the freedom to let go and not think about rules.

Before you go and get yourself a bikini wax or pack an overnight bag, it's a good idea to have a conversation about sex. In the spirit of being honest, standing in who we are, and practicing good communication, talking about sex before having it opens the door to a better connection and decreases the chances of misunderstandings.

Once you establish that you're in a relationship, have dealt with some obstacles, and have taken your relationship to the next level, coming out in public and to friends and family happens rather organically.

Coming Out (Farmers' Markets and Facebook)

After we had been dating for about a month or so, Cami asked me to meet her at the farmers' market one Sunday. As I went about my morning beforehand, cleaning my apartment, I began to get nervous. The farmers' market in my community was like a lesbian bar with cool straight people attending. Girls were everywhere. So on some level, going to the farmers' market with Cami, holding hands as we shopped for apples, felt like a big deal. Suddenly, stooped over the bathtub in my rubber gloves, I realized that Cami was making a statement: *We're together*. I grinned from ear to ear, even as my stomach rumbled with nerves.

I'm a big believer that secrets are bad, or at least a sign of something bad. In the past, secrets have been hurtful and toxic, both to me and to whomever I was keeping them from. If you want to keep your new girl a secret or vice versa, it might be time to consider whether this relationship is where you want to be.

When it comes to meeting friends, changing your Facebook status, and other coming-out-as-a-couple activities, these are all just more opportunities to communicate and have conversations about where we are. One word of caution: be careful to avoid making assumptions about what meeting her friends means. It doesn't necessarily mean she wants to be exclusive. This is all the more reason to have a clear conversation about it.

Moving In Together

When I was in my late twenties, I spent about nine months living at my mom's house. One August evening, I met and started dating Rori, who lived in a nearby city with her mom. I fell in love fast, and so did she. I couldn't put my finger on it, but I knew this was different. After five months of not so subtly sneaking into each other's rooms and meeting for rendezvous at nearby hotels, we decided to find an apartment together. In the end, Rori and I did move in together, and for five years we had what was, up until this point, the best, healthiest relationship I'd ever had.

Fast-forward seventeen years, and I found myself dating Vikki, whom I'd known for over a year and who was a close friend. When we moved in together after dating for five months or so, I thought it would be fine, just like before. But I realized very quickly that not only did we not know very much about each other, we lived very differently. When the relationship suddenly ended, I found myself looking for a place to live in a flooded rental market. The point is, if there's no right time to move in, how will we ever know when it *is* the right time? How can we tell the difference between the one that works out and the one where conflict begins the moment the boxes are unpacked?

Action Step: What I Did

Determined to identify whether we were ready to move in together or not, I tried the following:

I decided that going forward, I would need to be able to answer the following questions before I was ready to move in with someone again.

1. Are we both ready to take our relationship to a deeper commitment? Have we talked about what that means?
2. How will we divide expenses (mortgage or rent, utilities, etc.)?
3. How will we share housekeeping duties?

4. What are our pet peeves (dirty dishes in the sink, etc.)?
5. How much alone time do we each need? How will we communicate that?
6. What are our expectations about having guests or out-of-town visitors?
7. What has and has not worked with past roommates or girlfriends?
8. What are our expectations about checking in with each other at the end of the workday?
9. What do we each need when we've had a bad day? When we're sick? When we're angry or sad? How will we communicate that?
10. How will we divide duplicate household goods (furniture, dishes, electronics, etc.)?
11. What is most important to us about our home?

Sometimes, no matter how much love there may be or how hard we try, something just doesn't work. Part of taking extraordinary care of ourselves and staying in tune with our own needs is recognizing this fine line.

Letting Go and Moving On

Why is it that when it comes to relationships, we often hang on tighter even when evidence shows that there's just nothing left for us there? Since all relationships bring up issues, how do we know the difference between normal stuff and incompatibility stuff? I realized I'd hung in too long sometimes because of fear of failure. Or I got stuck in the details, such as that we were living together. Mostly, though, I stayed too long in relationships because I just didn't know how to know it was over.

Action Step: What I Did

Determined to identify signs that a relationship is over sooner, I tried the following:

After twenty years of staying too long at the party, I have identified four ways to know when a relationship is over.

1. **I'm hanging in out of nostalgia.**

   It is so confusing, when remembering the good times from early on, to accept that things have changed. Over time I learned that once I have tried everything else and am just holding on, hoping it will be the way it once was, or that things will change in the ways I need in order for the relationship to work for me, it is already over.

2. **I have lost things—friends, sleep, a sense of who I am.**

   Love shouldn't hurt or cause me to lose things. This has been such a hard thing for me to accept, as I feel there is a middle ground between "all relationships take work" and "love shouldn't hurt." What I realized is that for me, the key is loss. Once a pattern develops that involves my losing things—a sense of myself, focus on my career, sleep, etc.—the relationship has deteriorated into the unhealthy realm and it's time to cut my losses.

3. **One of us is stuck in victim mode.**

   Taking responsibility for ourselves takes courage and the ability to tolerate our own limitations. Whether due to a personality disorder, untreated addiction, or general immaturity, some people lack the capacity for taking responsibility at certain points in their lives. You can spot this in someone when you notice she will not say I'm sorry or when there is a chronic lack of awareness about how her behavior impacts you. I can't work with a blamer, someone unwilling to grow.

4. **Someone broke a deal breaker.**
   Things such as cheating, shutting down during conflict, punishing over a perceived wrong, lack of trust, or financial instability are deal breakers for me. Looking back, it's clear to me that once a deal breaker was cracked for either of us, it was a turning point in the relationship—one that should have indicated it was time to end it.

Action Step: What You Can Do
Grab a journal and complete your own action step.

1. Identify one relationship in which you felt you stayed too long.
2. Identify all the factors that were happening at the time (e.g., a loved one passed away, you just moved, etc.).
3. Examine what you felt and told yourself at the time to stay in the relationship.
4. To take it a step further, explore excuses you made that were really about you, not her (e.g., I told myself I stayed because her sister had passed away, but really I stayed because I didn't want to be alone).

I realized all of the signs come down to one thing. The solution for what to do lies in the answer to one question: *Am I compromising who I am?*

The thing about love is that it doesn't discriminate. We can love someone who is not at all compatible with us. Most of us have experienced loving someone who was actually bad for us. Dating successfully is dating that we learn from, whether the relationship works out in the long run or not. Marrianne Williamson once said that "failure is something you don't learn from. Success is when you learn." Successful dating requires having an open heart while maintaining a strong resolve that we will not settle for unhealthy love. Sometimes we have to decide that we deserve better than loving someone who isn't capable of loving us back in the ways we need. This courage requires letting love go.

A Note on Hard

While much of this chapter has been about how hard a relationship shouldn't be, that bucket of relationships is not to be confused with the bucket of normal hard times that arise in relationships. I have come to the conclusion that no matter whom we date, stuff will come up. Relationships are the places where old issues surface and where we have the opportunity to heal if we work on ourselves. Our old wounds and her old wounds will intertwine at times and cause conflict. I believe that this is normal and healthy in a deeply intimate relationship—it's the good hard. The bad hard requires us to compromise who we are or what we value in order to stay in the relationship.

Summary

After twenty years of dating and breakups, I learned that we're all just looking for connection. Maybe dating in modern times requires getting past our tendency to tune out and distract ourselves with being busy, using technology, and avoiding our feelings. I learned that what we focus on is the biggest currency we have. I set my intention to focus on what I do want, keep prioritizing myself, and approach dating with curiosity rather than judgment.

After all, by waking up in our own lives, by being present to the moment at hand, we protect ourselves from the blinders that love can induce and are more likely to enjoy dating. We are more apt to notice red flags, identify incompatibility, and end the relationship so we can move on to the right one. By taking responsibility for our part in past relationships, we empower ourselves to do a better job of taking care of ourselves going forward.

Late one afternoon, as I stood in front of the mirror, getting ready to go to a basketball game where I'd meet a girl I had come across online, it occurred to me that I didn't feel nervous. I checked myself for a moment. Was I meeting her because I was bored? Because she had asked? I considered both for a moment and shook my head. No. I was meeting her because she had asked, because she intrigued me, and because I was ready to meet people and date. I felt a surge of confidence in my ability to be honest, to be myself, and to spot red flags sooner. I smiled at this realization as I reached for the light switch and took once last glance in the mirror. I shrugged and lifted my shoulder in a sassy moment of fabulousness. As I turned off the kitchen light and locked my front door, I thought, *This. This is what you do after the breakup, before the next U-Haul. You put one foot in front of the other and just go.* If I could go back and sit down next to my old self, the heartbroken one with her legs splayed on the wood floor in front of the mixed-up shelves, I would tell her only one thing: *Stop looking for* her. *Look for* you.

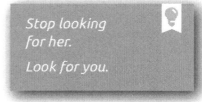

Appendix A

Quiz: How to Know If I'm Ready to Date

Am I Ready to Date?	
Open to connection	☐ Am I ready to open up to connection and vulnerability? ☐ Can I identify what works and doesn't work for me in relationships? ☐ Can I sit across from someone and think, *Are you a good fit for me?*
Self-confident	☐ Do I feel solid in who I am? ☐ Is my intention in dating to get to know someone in order to determine romantic compatibility? ☐ Can I accept rejection without taking it personally? ☐ Do I trust and listen to my intuition or gut instincts?
Commitment to taking extraordinary care of myself	☐ Am I at peace most of the time? ☐ Do I have my own goals, hobbies, and friends? ☐ Am I focused on myself and being my most authentic self?
Identified part in past relationships	☐ Have I identified my part in past relationships? ☐ Am I through the stages of grief (e.g., I'm not crying or sighing a lot, am eating and sleeping like normal, and am not angry or bitter)? ☐ Have I let go of and moved on from my exes?
Healthy boundaries	☐ Am I ready to identify what I want rather than what I don't want? ☐ Can I approach dating with curiosity rather than judgment? ☐ Do I cope well with life? When stress arises, do I deal with it in healthy ways or deflect it onto someone else?

Scoring
Mostly yes: You're ready! We are always evolving, and that's okay.

Half yes/half no: You're ready, but proceed with caution. Keep an eye out for your motivation (see good and not-so-good reasons for dating) and your approach (are you curious? focused on what you want rather than what you don't want?).

Mostly no: You're not quite ready yet. But don't be discouraged. By recognizing it's not yet time to date, you have the opportunity to spend some healthy time getting right with yourself and thus setting up your next relationship to be the healthiest one yet!

Appendix B

Sample Online Dating Profile

I am down to earth, active, kind, intelligent, and genuine. I guess I'm considered a lipstick lesbian, though I'm athletic and have been told I'm low maintenance. Plus I generally dislike labels. The best way to describe me is a mix of contradictions (which I like to think of as making me a well-rounded person).

I am outgoing, but I value time alone just as much. I am active, but I prioritize rest and meditation. I view fashion as art, and I can most often be found in my running shoes and jeans. I care about the environment, and I often wear makeup (cruelty free). I am a total foodie and eat healthy most of the time. I am successful and goal oriented, and I recognize that what I do for a living falls last in place in defining me. I love hip-hop music and show tunes. I often watch documentaries and horrible reality TV. I enjoy going out dancing or for dinner, and I love staying home in sweats. I love girls who have a sense of humor and can be serious. I am graceful when dancing and clumsy every other moment. I love routine, and I'm told I am spontaneous. I am a bit of a clean freak when it comes to my home, but am endlessly messy when it comes to spilling things on myself. I am good at keeping people's secrets and respecting privacy, but I rarely keep secrets of my own. I am a caregiver at heart and hopelessly independent and self-sufficient. I am passionate and surprisingly level-headed, especially in a crisis. I am friendly and social, but I do best in smaller groups or one-on-one. I love to host parties and plan events and sometimes don't want to make any decisions at all. I hate driving but love travel. I'm an academic and am prone to laughing aloud at stupid comedy movies. I am open and pensive. Honest and tactful. Serious and silly. Strong and soft.

I am looking for the one. However, I am just getting back out there after a breakup, so I'm interested in meeting new people and getting to know someone first. I love women who are athletic, kind, professional, confident, in touch with their emotions, honest, *always growing, and who are good communicators.* I am fiercely independent and also extremely committed when I'm with someone, so I do best with women who are confident but also capable of consistent emotional intimacy. I don't play games. I don't lie or have a personality or mental disorder. I have dealt with my childhood and am over my exes. I don't escape to deal with life. I am professional, successful, and busy, and I have a wonderful support group of friends and family. I have been lucky in love and have dated some amazing women. While those relationships didn't work out in the long run, I learned a lot about myself and about relationships in general. While I will forever be growing and learning, I have never been more ready to settle down with the right person.

Appendix C

Other Cautionary Tales

The Big-Gesture Girl

Vikki was a big-gesture girl, a charmer. A good way to tell the difference between a genuine romantic girl and a big-gesture girl is in her own attitude about the gesture. For example, when Vikki did something romantic such as cooking dinner, her focus was solely on pointing out how much trouble she'd gone to and making it seem as if I wasn't grateful enough. Sometimes she would actually say, "See, I'm a good girlfriend." There's nothing inherently wrong with wooing behavior—it may just be enthusiasm. I have learned to just note it and watch it over time. Insincere gestures are not sustainable and will eventually get thrown back in your face (e.g., in the middle of a disagreement, she shouts, "But I made you dinner!").

The You'll-Do Girl

I didn't know it at the time, but Anna was the you'll-do girl. You'll-do girls just want a girlfriend. They often have no boundaries in terms of the stages of a relationship. You go on one date, and she wants to settle down. In my experience, the biggest sign of a you'll-do, desperate girl is that she asks very few questions about you. I wanted to believe Anna was into me, but she would have dated anyone. It was never about me or how compatible we were.

It was about having someone. Anyone. If you get the feeling that her attitude is "you'll do," you've found yourself in the presence of a desperate you'll-do girl.

The Detached Girl

The player girl fits here, as being a player is less about getting girls and more about the detachment with which she does it. She can get anyone's number in a bar and is proud of it. But she's even more proud of the way she can date multiple girls without truly connecting to any of them. She boasts that she's not really responsible if girls fall for her—she's straight with them about not wanting a relationship, after all.

The Bait-and-Switch Girl

The bait-and-switch girl may be the most confusing of all. You think you are dating Person A, and then wham! Person B shows up, and you're standing in your tracks looking for Person A and wondering what you missed. This has two parts to it: the giving and the receiving. For example, if someone presents herself one way and is fairly consistent about that in her actions early on but then changes on you, then she has given you the bait and switch. Sometimes, though, we fail to recognize the truth of who someone is because of our own unwillingness to see her for who she is. We dismiss behaviors, don't ask questions when we don't understand something, or don't speak up for ourselves. This difference comes back to red flags and getting better at seeing people for who they are.

In my experience, most of these behaviors are rather harmless, and it's just a matter of identifying what works and doesn't work for us. It comes down to choosing a partner who is capable of coping, managing stress, growing, and walking with us on this journey, no matter what it brings.

References

Behrendt, G. & A. Ruotola. *It's Called a Breakup Because It's Broken.* New York: Broadway Books, 2005.

Behrendt, G. & L. Tuccillo. *He's Just Not That Into You.* New York: Simon Spotlight Entertainment, 2004.

Brown, B. *The Gifts of Imperfection.* Center City, MN: Hazelden, 2010.

Brown, S. L. *Women Who Love Psychopaths: Inside the Relationships of Inevitable Harm with Psychopaths, Sociopaths & Narcissists.* Mask Publishing, 2010.

Burton, N., J. Fishman, & M. McCrary. *The Little Black Book of Big Red Flags: Relationship Warning Signs.* Avon, MA: Adams Media, 2011.

Elliot, S. J. *Getting Past Your Breakup.* Cambridge, MA: Da Capo Press, 2009.

Kabat-Zinn, J. *Coming to Our Senses: Healing Ourselves and the World through Mindfulness.* New York: Hyperion, 2006.

Lamott, A. *Bird by Bird: Some Instructions on Writing and Life.* New York: First Anchor Books, 1995.

Malia, Mary. www.gaygirldatingcoach.com.

Marshall, B. *Deal Breakers.* New York: Simon Spotlight Entertainment, 2007.

Nepo, M. *The Book of Awakening: Having the Life You Want by Being Present to the Life You Have*. San Francisco, CA: Conari Press, 2000.

Oprah.com (2015). *Living the Law of Attraction*. Retrieved from http://www.oprah.com/spirit/The-Law-of-Attraction-Real-Life-Stories_1/1

Schwartz, R. L. & M. Murrain. *Conscious Lesbian Dating & Love: A Twelve-Week Roadmap for Finding the Right Partner, Being the Right Partner, and Creating the Relationship of Your Dreams*. Oakland, CA: Six Directions Press, 2015.